Ultimate Aptitude Tests

Jim Barrett
Tom Barrett

Ultimate
Aptitude
Tests

Over **1000** practice
questions for abstract
visual, numerical, verbal,
physical, spatial and
systems tests

FOURTH EDITION

KoganPage

Publisher's note

Every possible effort has been made to ensure that the information contained in this book is accurate at the time of going to press, and the publishers and authors cannot accept responsibility for any errors or omissions, however caused. No responsibility for loss or damage occasioned to any person acting, or refraining from action, as a result of the material in this publication can be accepted by the editor, the publisher or the authors.

Some of the tests included in this book have previously been included in *Aptitude, Personality and Motivation Tests* (2004), *How to Pass Advanced Aptitude Tests* (2008) and *The Aptitude Workbook* (2008) published by Kogan Page.

First published in Great Britain and the United States in 2008 by Kogan Page Limited
Second edition 2012
Third edition 2015
Fourth edition 2018

2nd Floor, 45 Gee Street	c/o Martin P Hill Consulting	4737/23 Ansari Road
London	122 W 27th Street	Daryaganj
EC1V 3RS	New York, NY 10001	New Delhi 110002
United Kingdom	USA	India

www.koganpage.com

ISBN   978 0 7494 8208 4
EISBN   978 0 7494 8209 1

British Library Cataloguing-in-Publication Data

A CIP record for this book is available from the British Library.

Typeset by Integra Software Services, Pondicherry
Print production managed by Jellyfish
Printed and bound by CPI Group (UK) Ltd, Croydon, CR0 4YY

CONTENTS

INTRODUCTION

The aptitude tests in this book are wide ranging and cover the types of tests found in 'real' assessment and selection situations. They are suited to people at secondary school, college and in employment.

What are aptitude tests?

Aptitude tests aim to measure the direction and power of a person's intelligence. Properly devised aptitude tests like those in this book use scientific methods to ensure consistency of results and accurate comparison of one result with another. You can then predict what your competencies are likely to be. Obviously, if a test is not predictive there is little point in using it.

When and why are aptitude tests used?

It is becoming routine for organizations to use tests to select externally as well as internally. Why internally, when you might suppose that a person's abilities and characteristics are already well known? Here are some of the advantages:

- to create awareness of further potential for development in the person's present job;
- as a means of assessing suitability for alternative functional opportunities within the same organization;

- in competition with external applicants, to deliberately 'test the market', that is, to ensure that the quality of internal staff is keeping pace with what is happening in other, possibly rival, organizations;
- as a way of validating training programmes;
- for purposes of career guidance and counselling.

Why are aptitude tests useful?

Aptitude tests are just like any other tools that can increase efficiency and productivity. There is substantial risk attached to selecting or developing people who turn out to be unsuitable, and the financial costs attached to wrong decisions about employment can be considerable.

Testing enables many of the aims of organizations that, ultimately, are to do with getting the best results from their people, for example:

- to obtain the most competent students or staff and to develop that competence in order to make fullest use of each person's contribution;
- to reduce the risk of people leaving, since it makes sense to develop staff, where possible, if they have talents that can be extended;
- to be proactive in discovering potential in staff who may not be aware of it themselves;
- to develop relevant training programmes, either because the tests check on the effectiveness of training or because they help to make sure that training is directed at those most likely to benefit from it;
- to obtain increased staff satisfaction as the result of using tests, since they are not used to judge performance in the present job, but to reveal possible opportunities.

So, provided aptitude tests are used properly there is 'nothing to lose, but everything to gain' by the use of tests.

Anything that will decrease costs and increase the probability of success will be taken seriously by an organization. This has led many organizations to investigate numerous methods, including graphology and astrology, but it is only the psychometric test method that can be shown to be consistently accurate, going beyond guesswork or 'gazing into a crystal ball'!

How accurate are the tests?

Predictive validity simply asks whether any kind of test, assertion or forecast is accurate. A ruler is a common measure of scale; a ruler measures distances of height, length or width. In the case of aptitude tests, the type of ruler used is a scale to measure *validity*.

The scale of *validity* is said to be zero if a forecast is correct only 50 per cent of the time. This is equivalent to 'tossing a coin' and obtaining heads or tails. If you could predict accurately every time the coin was tossed whether it would land heads or tails, then you would be predicting with perfect accuracy. In this case the *validity* would be 100 per cent.

Any test or forecast that is better than chance may be useful. That is why we ask the advice of people we presume to be wise; as they have 'done it before' we hope they will increase our chances of making a good choice. The trouble with using a 'wise person' is, of course, that what they say is not scientific, whatever skill they have being limited to their own experience.

It is very difficult indeed to obtain a perfect prediction, though in some sciences and industries we are shocked when we learn that predictions are imperfect. For example, a prediction that an aircraft will not crash is very close to 100 per cent. Aircraft safety needs to be an almost-perfect prediction as we would probably not ride in an aircraft if we thought that it had any chance of crashing. In fact, *predictive validity* in this area is so high that most of us can put it out of our minds. Yet, unfortunately, crashes occur, reminding us that we do have to live with less-than perfect prediction in this world.

Predicting human performance is extremely complicated, much more difficult than predicting what will happen to machines. This is why predictions based upon tests, even those that are well researched, commonly fall well short of a perfect 100 per cent. This may be for two reasons: 1) there may be circumstances related to the test itself, including its administration or interpretation that undermine its predictive value; 2) there may be circumstances around the person, or subject, who has taken the test that alter the chance of the test being predictive, such as altered social or emotional circumstances.

Among selection devices, graphology, astrology and similar methods are no better than chance. Although individuals who claim to have special insight or powers of divination have been employed by organizations to help make selection of staff, their success has probably depended more on their intuition as an interviewer than any valid method in their prognostications. In contrast, aptitude tests are:

- an efficient way of collecting information;
- objective, as the information is difficult to obtain by any other method; for example, where an interview question might be 'How good is your maths?', a test score can say precisely how good a person is;

- comparative: individuals can be compared directly with a relevant group;
- a better way of predicting success or satisfaction at various jobs than other selection devices.

What do the tests measure?

The psychometric tests used in this book have a number of advantages. They give an indication of abstract and practical mental capacity in six significant areas. They are varied enough to give an indication of potential as well as present attainment. As they have been standardized on the same population it is possible to obtain an estimate of how much better, or worse, you may be on one test as opposed to another.

It is obvious that people do have aptitudes that lead them to become better in one area of study or area of work than others. No other explanation fits our observation of the range and diversity of talent people have and why, in our own case, we know we have strengths and weaknesses.

Most people are aware of their strengths and weaknesses, but often over- or underestimate themselves. Sometimes they have never had cause to use a particular talent and thus have never become aware that it lies dormant in them. Organizations may also use tests to establish the presence of characteristics they think are important because they distrust conventional examination results or do not think that those results are appropriate for various reasons.

It is worth remembering that tests of one kind or another are being used all the time, as we constantly judge people against our experience. Sometimes we get it right, sometimes we don't. Tests should help us to get it right more often, though nothing can ever be asserted with complete finality.

What it is possible to do with psychometric tests is to assert a probability, for example the probability that a particular event will happen is less than one in a hundred or one in a thousand, and so on. This is the nature of both statistics and human potential, where we are dealing with probabilities, not certainties.

Therefore, we have to try to estimate how certain, or uncertain, we are when we use tests. For example, just because someone has not obtained a certain level on a test, it does not mean that they cannot succeed in a particular job. So, how likely is it that an individual might succeed or fail? If it can be shown that only 5 per cent of people who obtain a particular score are likely to be successful, then an organization may be justified in giving the job to someone who has a 95 per cent chance of being successful.

What is the difference between 'aptitudes' and 'abilities'?

Aptitudes should not be confused with abilities. Present skills and capabilities are not aptitudes. Aptitudes are about 'potential', which is not necessarily realized at the present time. It is like a natural intelligence. Many tests show a mixture of both ability and aptitude – ability to understand what the test requires and aptitude to perform at something for which a person may not as yet have any prior experience.

It is reasonable to measure aptitude only when it is assumed that people taking the test have had sufficient chance to develop the same ability. For example, there would be little point in giving a test of English vocabulary to a candidate who spoke very little English if all the other candidates were native English speakers. On the other hand, such tests are routinely used in teaching English as a foreign language, where applicants' level of English needs to be known.

Where ability is not required and testers want to look at some form of potential that may be exploited, tests become more abstract, for example reducing the need for vocabulary or numerical skills. This is how aptitude tests discover people with potential beyond the skills that have emerged thus far!

In summary, aptitude tests allow us to:

- Look at potential in a similar way for everybody. They attempt to put everybody on an 'equal playing field'. Even though there may never be such a thing, because life is rarely like that, there are advantages in seeing what happens when we try.
- They are a way of attempting to 'take stock' of something that is usually affected, contaminated and distorted by so many other variables, in particular educational disadvantage or prejudice.
- They are a means of trying to ensure that there is some opportunity for people to demonstrate the resources they have.
- They can investigate whether there is potential that people are not aware of. Often, the discovery of potential leads to the development of new interests or a fuller personal realization.

Comparing your aptitude on different tests

An individual's aptitudes only make sense in relation to others. Therefore, the tests in this book have been devised, using standard procedures, to compare you as far as possible with everybody else. Otherwise, you cannot say with any certainty that you are better at words than numbers.

You also have to make sure certain conditions are met so that the tests work as accurately as possible and to give yourself the same chance as everybody else. This is not literally possible; no two people can ever be in exactly the same situation when they are tested: there are just too many physical, social and emotional variables. However, as far as possible, disadvantageous factors must be removed. For example, make sure you:

- are not distracted;
- are comfortable;
- are prepared;
- are clear about the instructions;
- are timed accurately;
- have the necessary external resources;
- are treated as fairly as everyone else.

There is a case for saying that the situation in which the same test is taken is almost bound to be unique, as it may be impossible to nullify the effect of so many variables. However, you must do the best you can.

You can think of reducing many of the major adverse variables yourself, such as poor lighting, cramped conditions, intimidation and so on, but you cannot always think of everything. Therefore, it is wise to prepare for testing in advance by dealing with anything that might be distracting and making sure that you have everything you need to do the test.

Interpreting your test results

Proper interpretation of tests is the province of an expert, someone who knows how the test must be administered, knows about the test itself and what test scores mean, and has had sufficient practice in using tests. However, this book is designed to assist you to use them properly so that you can obtain meaningful results from doing them. Notes on the purpose of each test precede each section. At the end of the book you will find instructions and a chart to assist you in calculating your intelligence quotient or IQ. With this information you will be able to gain some insight into your intellectual strengths and how you may be able to use them.

Part One
Abstract visual tests

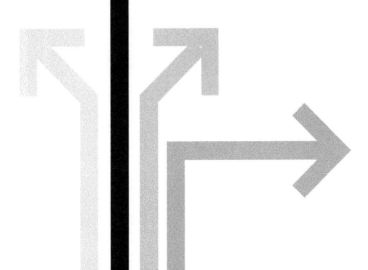

The three tests in this section are of a type long regarded as being the 'purest' means of measuring basic intelligence, that is, the natural ability you were born with. This is because the tests are only minimally dependent upon prior learning or past skills. In particular, there is no verbal or numerical processing involved. They are thus good indicators of whether a person's educational attainments are keeping pace with the level of potential indicated by the level shown on these tests. If not, it will often be worth using remedial or training programmes to raise a person's performance to the level that the measure of their basic intelligence indicates they are capable of.

Test 1, Constructs, measures an aptitude for seeing around things, from different angles and sides and in different ways. Put like this, you may appreciate that these qualities are relevant to a broad spectrum of careers demanding intellectual flexibility and depth. For reasons that are not fully understood, people with this type of ability are usually as good at working out social issues as they are factual ones.

Test 2, Sequences, does not have the multidimensional element of Constructs, but it requires a more linear, logical approach. An intensity of concentration is required to maintain the thread of clues in order to arrive at the end result. Like the other tests in this section, Sequences is a demanding task often revealing a long-term potential that may not be apparent in a young person but comes out in adulthood.

Test 3, Perceptual, requires a deductive approach to problem solving, an aptitude for grasping the situation and organizing its essential elements in order to draw a conclusion. People who do well on this test often have a leaning towards science, including social science, possibly because it highlights their ability in handling abstract relevant information.

TEST 1

CONSTRUCTS

In this test you have to imagine how a design would look when it is folded up to make a cube (or box). In each case you are given a plan of an unfolded cube and your job is to fold it together 'in your mind'. For example:

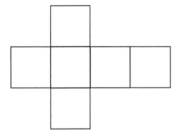

becomes

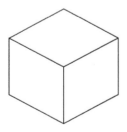

To the right of each plan, you are shown four cubes. For each item, write 'Y' for Yes or mark a tick if you think the cube is made from the plan, and write 'N' for No or make a cross if you think it could not be made from the plan. If you want to change your answer, rub out and clearly tick your preference. Examples 1) and 2) have been done to show you how. If this is not your book, please mark your answers on a separate sheet of paper.

Example 1

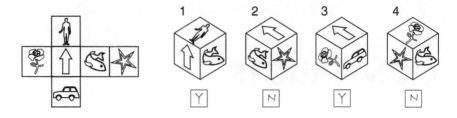

Example 2

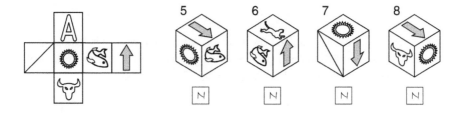

If you want, you can have paper and a pencil ready in case you want to draw out the figures. You have to work as quickly and as accurately as you can. Remember, if this is not your book, record your answers on a separate sheet of paper. Timing yourself on this test will give you the best estimate of your aptitude and allows the most accurate comparison between your results and those of others, as well as comparing your performance on other tests. If you are doing the test only to gain familiarity with this type of test you can, of course, spend as much time as you like on the test.

Timed test: 8 minutes

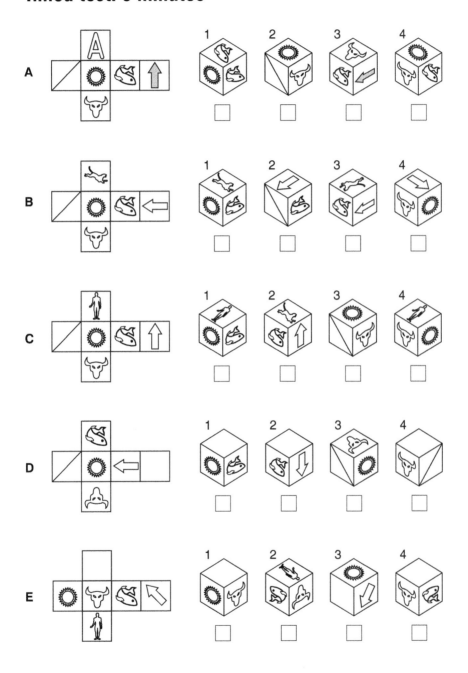

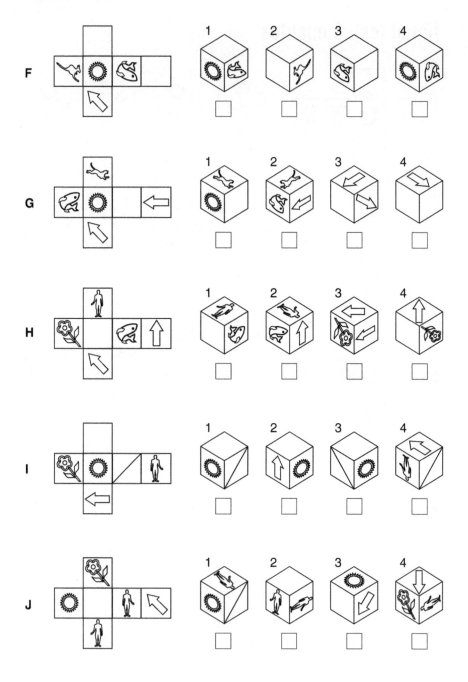

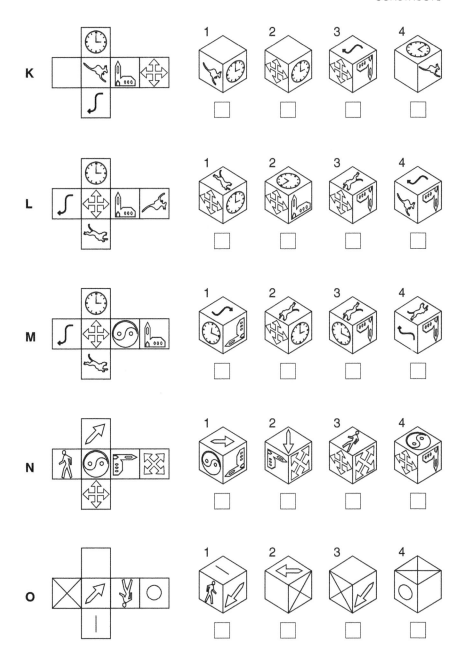

K

L

M

N

O

Answers

A	1. N	2. Y	3. N	4. Y
B	1. Y	2. N	3. N	4. N
C	1. Y	2. N	3. Y	4. N
D	1. N	2. Y	3. N	4. N
E	1. Y	2. Y	3. Y	4. N
F	1. Y	2. N	3. Y	4. N
G	1. Y	2. N	3. Y	4. N
H	1. N	2. Y	3. N	4. N
I	1. Y	2. N	3. N	4. Y
J	1. N	2. Y	3. N	4. Y
K	1. N	2. N	3. Y	4. N
L	1. N	2. N	3. N	4. N
M	1. N	2. N	3. N	4. N
N	1. N	2. Y	3. N	4. N
O	1. Y	2. Y	3. N	4. N

Scoring

Number right minus number wrong = _____

Plus 4 aged under 16, plus 2 if aged 17–20   + _____

Score on the test = _____

Use the following table to convert your test score to a score out of 10 or 'sten score'. You can then enter your 'sten score' in the chart on page 214.

Test score	1–15	16–20	21–25	26–30	31–35	36–40	41–43	44–46	47–49	50+
Sten score	1	2	3	4	5	6	7	8	9	10

TEST 2

SEQUENCES

You are given a string of shapes. You have to work out which two shapes are missing from the string. The missing shapes have been replaced with a 1 and a 2. Choose the correct answers from the possible answers provided on the page. Write in the correct letter which goes with the missing shape. There is space to write in your answers on the right of the page.

Possible answers:

Example 1

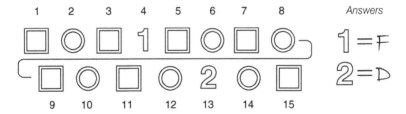

								Answers
								1 = F
								2 = D

Example 2

Answers

1 = A

2 = F

In Example 1, there is a sequence of alternate squares and circles. The fourth in the sequence is a missing circle, so F is correct from the possible answers. Number 13 in the sequence, where a 2 has been placed, should have a square, so the correct answer is D.

In Example 2, the sequence is triangle, circle, square. A small, white circle would go where the 1 has been placed, so the correct answer is A. In the sequence, the circles are alternately small and large. A large circle would go where the 2 has been placed, so the correct answer is F.

The real test is done in just this way. Find the correct answer from those given on each page and write the letter in the space provided for answers. Both parts must be correct to score.

Do not mark this book if it is not your own, but record your answers and any working out you need to do on separate paper. If you wish to get an accurate idea of your aptitude, record the number of the question you are on after exactly 15 minutes. Otherwise, take as long as you wish to complete the items.

Timed test: 15 minutes

A   B   C   D   E   F

1   *1   2   3   4   5   6   7   8*

1 =
2 =

   9   10   11   12   13   14   15

2

1 =
2 =

3

1 =
2 =

4

1 =
2 =

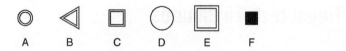

A   B   C   D   E   F

5   1 =
2 =

6   1 =
2 =

7   1 =
2 =

8   1 =
2 =

A   B   C   D   E   F   G   H   I

9

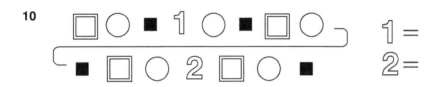

1 =
2 =

10

1 =
2 =

11

1 =
2 =

12

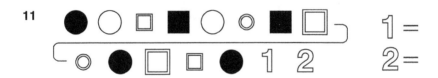

1 =
2 =

A   B   C   D   E   F   G   H   I   J   K   L

13

1 =
2 =

14

1 =
2 =

15

1 =
2 =

16

1 =
2 =

17   ■ ○ □ ■ □ ○ 1 □
□ 2 □ □ ■

1 =
2 =

18   △ ■ ○ △ △ ■ 1
△ 2 ■ ○ △

1 =
2 =

19   ■ △ 1 ○ ■ △ □ ○
■ △ □ ○ 2 △

1 =
2 =

20   ○ △ ■ 1 ○ △ □ ●
2 △ □ ○ ● △

1 =
2 =

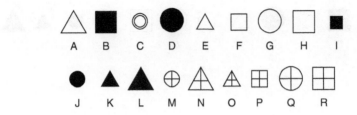

21   △ ◎ 1 ■ △ ◎ □ □ ⌐ 1 =
          ▲ 2 □ □ △   2 =

22   1 △ ▪ ○ △ △ ■ ○ ⌐ 1 =
          △ △ ■ 2 △   2 =

23   ▲ □ ○ △ 1 □ ◦ ⌐ 1 =
          △ ▲ □ ◎ 2 ▲ □   2 =

24   ○ ⊕ ▪ ▲ ○ ◎ ⊞ ▲ ⌐ 1 =
          ● 1 □ 2 ● ● □ △   2 =

SEQUENCES **23**

25

○ △ ▪ ⟁ ◎ △ 1

▲ 2 △ □ △

1 =

2 =

26

○ ■ ▪ ○ ○ 1 ■

○ ◎ ■ 2 ◎ ○

1 =

2 =

27

1 □ ○ ▪ ▲ □ ◎

□ △ □ ● ▪ △ 2

1 =

2 =

28

⊕ □ ● ▪ △ ⊕ □

● ▪ △ ⊕ 1 2

1 =

2 =

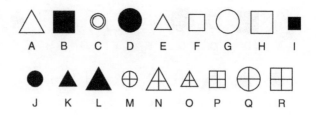

29 ■ △ ◎ ○ ⟁ □ ▲ 1 ⌐
   ◎ △ ⊞ △ 2 ◎ △   1 =
                              2 =

30 △ 1 ▪ ○ ⊕ △ ■ ■ ⌐
   ◎ ⊕ △ ▪ ■ ○ 2   1 =
                              2 =

31 1 ● □ ○ ⊞ △ ◎ □ ● ⌐
   □ △ ⊕ 2 ◎ □ ▲ ○   1 =
                              2 =

32 1 △ ● ⊕ ▪ △ ● ⌐
   ⊕ ■ △ ● ⊕ 2   1 =
                              2 =

Answers

1 1 = E, 2 = D	**9** 1 = B, 2 = G	**17** 1 = B, 2 = J	**25** 1 = F, 2 = M
2 1 = C, 2 = D	**10** 1 = F, 2 = G	**18** 1 = G, 2 = A	**26** 1 = I, 2 = B
3 1 = A, 2 = C	**11** 1 = B, 2 = D	**19** 1 = F, 2 = B	**27** 1 = E, 2 = H
4 1 = C, 2 = F	**12** 1 = A, 2 = I	**20** 1 = G, 2 = G	**28** 1 = F, 2 = J
5 1 = B, 2 = E	**13** 1 = H, 2 = I	**21** 1 = H, 2 = C	**29** 1 = C, 2 = J
6 1 = E, 2 = F	**14** 1 = I, 2 = A	**22** 1 = A, 2 = C	**30** 1 = B, 2 = M
7 1 = C, 2 = E	**15** 1 = D, 2 = E	**23** 1 = K, 2 = A	**31** 1 = E, 2 = F
8 1 = D, 2 = A	**16** 1 = G, 2 = H	**24** 1 = G, 2 = O	**32** 1 = I, 2 = I

Scoring

Number right minus number wrong = _____

Plus 3 aged under 16, plus 1 if aged 17–20   + _____

Score on the test = _____

Use the following table to convert your test score to a score out of 10 or 'sten score'. You can then enter your 'sten score' in the chart on page 234.

Test score	1–2	3–5	6–8	9–10	11–12	13–14	15–18	19–21	22–24	25+
Sten score	1	2	3	4	5	6	7	8	9	10

Explanations

1   Large square – large circle, thus 1 is a large square, 2 is a large circle.

2   Triangle – large circle – small white square, thus 1 is a small white square and 2 is a large circle.

3   Small white circle – two small white squares, thus 1 is a small white circle and 2 is a small white square.

4   Small white square – small white circle – small black square, thus 1 is a small white square and 2 is a small black square.

5   Large white triangle – large white circle – large white square, thus 1 is a large white triangle and 2 is a large white square.

6   Large white square – large white circle – small black square, thus 1 is a large white square and 2 is a small black square.

7   Small white square – large white circle – small white square – large white square – small white circle – large white square, thus 1 is a small white square and 2 is a large white square.

8   Two large white circles – small black square – two small white circles, thus 1 is a large white circle and 2 is a small white circle.

9   Small black square – large white circle – large white square, thus 1 is a large white circle and 2 is a small black square.

10   Large white square – large white circle – small black square, thus 1 is a large white square and 2 is a small black square.

11   Two large – one small, thus 1 is large and 2 is small
     One black – two white, thus 1 is white and 2 is white
     Two circles – two squares, thus 1 is a circle and 2 is a square.

12   Three large – one small, thus 1 is small and 2 is large
     Two white – two black, thus 1 is white and 2 is black
     Three circles – one square, thus 1 is a circle and 2 is a square.

13   Two large – two small, thus 1 is large and 2 is small
     Two white – two black, thus 1 is white and 2 is black
     Squares, thus both 1 and 2 are squares.

14   Two large – two small, thus 1 is small and 2 is large
     Two white – two black, thus 1 is black and 2 is white
     Triangle – circle – square – square, thus 1 is a square and 2 is a triangle.

15   One small – three large, thus 1 is large and 2 is small
     Two black – two white, thus 1 is black and 2 is white
     Triangle – square – two circles, thus 1 is a circle and 2 a triangle.

16   Two large – two small, thus 1 is large and 2 is large
     One black – seven white, thus 1 is white and 2 is white
     Square – circle – triangle – circle, thus 1 is a circle and 2 is a square.

17   Three small – one large, thus 1 is large and 2 is small
     One black – two white, thus 1 is black and 2 is black
     Three squares – one circle, thus 1 is a square and 2 is a circle.

18   Three large – one small, thus 1 is large and 2 is large
     Three white – one black, thus 1 is white and 2 is white
     Square – circle – two triangles, thus 1 is a circle and 2 is a triangle.

19   One large – two small, thus 1 is small and 2 is large
     One black – three white, thus 1 is white and 2 is black
     Circle – square – triangle – square, thus 1 is a square and 2 is a square.

20   Three small – two large, thus 1 is large and 2 is large
     One black – four white, thus 1 is white and 2 is white
     Two circles – triangle – square, thus 1 is a circle and 2 is a circle.

21   One large – one small, thus 1 is large and 2 is small
     One black – four white, thus 1 is white and 2 is white
     Triangle – circle – two squares, thus 1 is a square and 2 is a circle.

22   Two large – one small, thus 1 is large and 2 is small
One black – three white, thus 1 is white and 2 is white
Two triangles – square – circle, thus 1 is a triangle and 2 is a circle.

23   Two small – one large, thus 1 is small and 2 is large
One black – three white, thus 1 is black and 2 is white
Two triangles – square – circle, thus 1 is a triangle and 2 is a triangle.

24   One large – then three or four small, thus 1 is large and 2 is small
Two white – cross-hatched – two black, thus 1 is white and 2 is cross-hatched
Two circles – square – triangle, thus 1 is a circle and 2 is a triangle.

25   One large – three small, thus 1 is small and 2 is small
Three white – black – cross-hatched, thus 1 is white and 2 is cross-hatched
Circle – triangle – square – triangle, thus 1 is a square and 2 is a circle.

26   Two large – one small, thus 1 is small and 2 is large
Two white – two black, thus 1 is black and 2 is black
Two circles – two squares, thus 1 is a square and 2 is a square.

27   Two large – four small, thus 1 is small and 2 is large
Four white – two black, thus 1 is white and 2 is white
Square – circle – square – triangle, thus 1 is a triangle and 2 is a square.

28   One large – three small, thus 1 is small and 2 is small
Two black – white – cross-hatched – white, thus 1 is white and 2 is black
Circle – square – circle – square – triangle, thus 1 is a square and 2 is a circle.

29   Two large – three small, thus 1 is small and 2 is small
One black – three white – cross-hatched – white, thus 1 is white and 2 is black
Square – triangle – two circles – triangle, thus 1 is a circle and 2 is a circle.

30   Two large – one small, thus 1 is large and 2 is small
Two black – white – cross-hatched – white, thus 1 is black and 2 is cross-hatched
Two squares – two circles – triangle, thus 1 is a square and 2 is a circle.

31   Two large – four small, thus 1 is small and 2 is small
Black – two white – cross-hatched – three white, thus 1 is white and 2 is white
Circle – square – circle – square – triangle, thus 1 is a triangle and 2 is a square.

32   Large – two small, thus 1 is small and 2 is small
White – black – cross-hatched – black, thus 1 is black and 2 is black
Triangle – two circles – square, thus 1 is a square and 2 is a square.

TEST 3

PERCEPTUAL

There are two types of problem in this test. In one type, you have to decide which of the objects is the 'odd one out'. In the second type you are shown a sequence of objects or shapes. Your task is to choose, from the alternatives you are given, the one that would come next in line.

Example 1

Which is the odd one out?

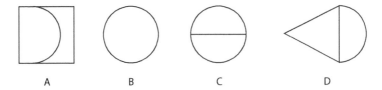

A	B	C	D

Example 2

Which comes next in the top line?

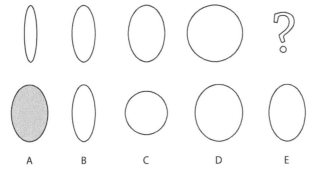

A	B	C	D	E

In Example 1, B is the correct answer. It is the only curved shape that does not also have a straight line.

In Example 2, the figures are of a circle that is turning. The figures can also be seen as a shape that is expanding by equal amounts until it becomes a full circle. The next step would be for the circle to turn by the same amount as before, or to decrease by the same amount as before. E is the correct answer. Although A is the correct shape, there is no reason why it should be shaded. D is not quite the correct size because it has not turned enough. B is not correct because it has turned too much. C is the wrong size and has not turned at all.

Do not mark this book if it is not your own, but record your answers and any working out you need to do on separate paper. If you wish to estimate your aptitude, record the number of the question you are on after exactly 10 minutes. Otherwise, take as long as you wish to complete the items.

Timed test: 10 minutes

1   Which is the odd one out?

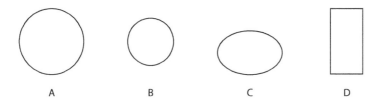

A   B   C   D

2   Which comes next?

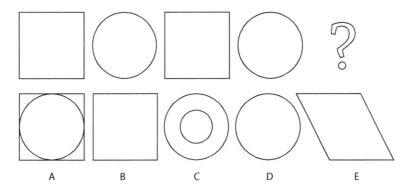

A   B   C   D   E

3   Which is the odd one out?

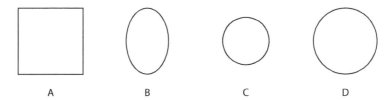

A   B   C   D

4   Which comes next?

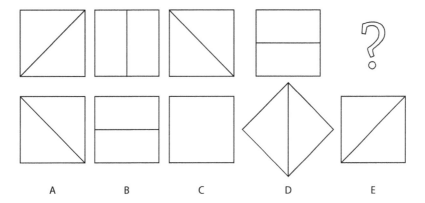

A   B   C   D   E

5 Which is the odd one out?

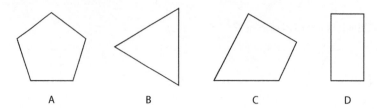

A   B   C   D

6 Which comes next?

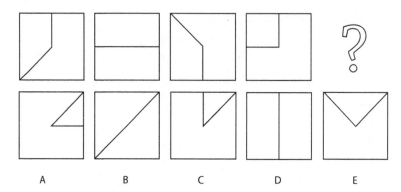

A   B   C   D   E

7 Which is the odd one out?

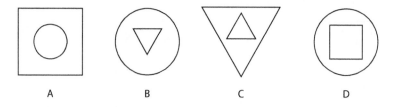

A   B   C   D

8 Which comes next?

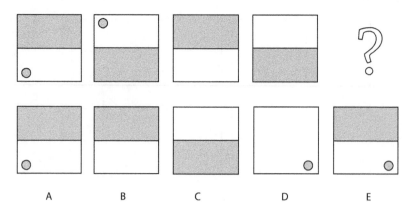

A   B   C   D   E

9   Which is the odd one out?

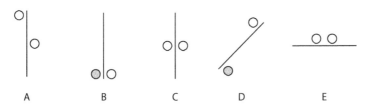

A   B   C   D   E

10   Which comes next?

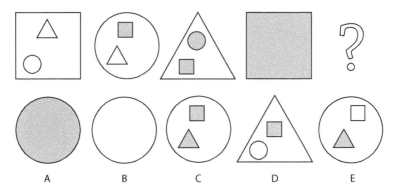

A   B   C   D   E

11   Which is the odd one out?

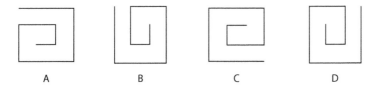

A   B   C   D

12   Which comes next?

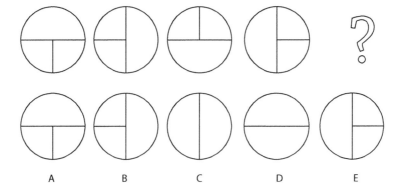

A   B   C   D   E

13 Which is the odd one out?

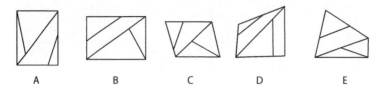

A   B   C   D   E

14 Which comes next?

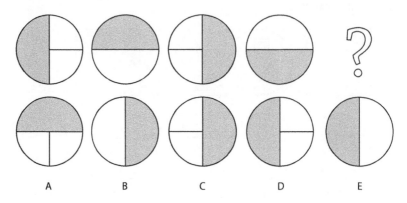

A   B   C   D   E

15 Which is the odd one out?

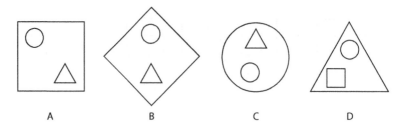

A   B   C   D

16 Which comes next?

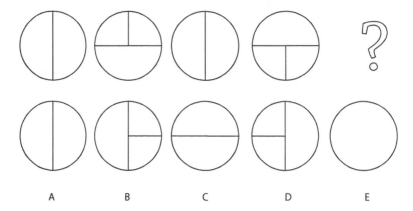

A   B   C   D   E

17 Which is the odd one out?

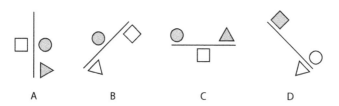

A   B   C   D

18 Which comes next?

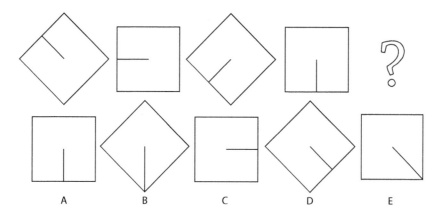

A   B   C   D   E

19 Which is the odd one out?

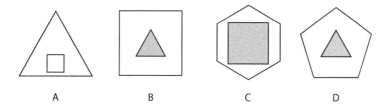

A   B   C   D

20 Which comes next?

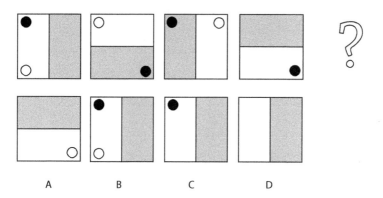

A   B   C   D

21   Which is the odd one out?

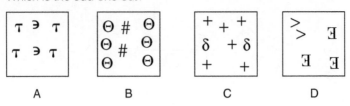

A   B   C   D

22   Which comes next?

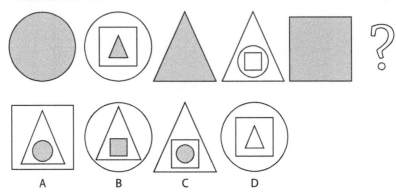

A   B   C   D

23   Which is the odd one out?

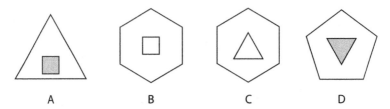

A   B   C   D

24   Which comes next?

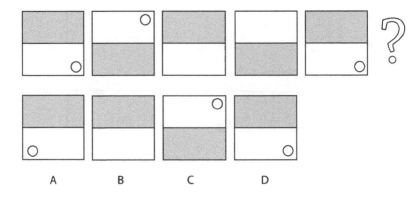

A   B   C   D

25   Which is the odd one out?

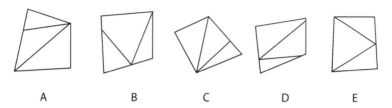

A   B   C   D   E

26   Which comes next?

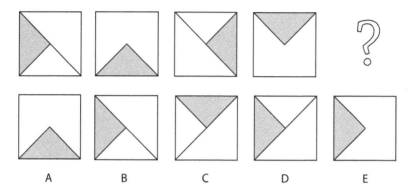

A   B   C   D   E

27   Which is the odd one out?

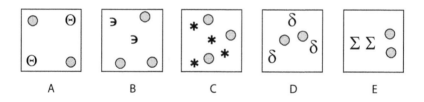

A   B   C   D   E

28   Which comes next?

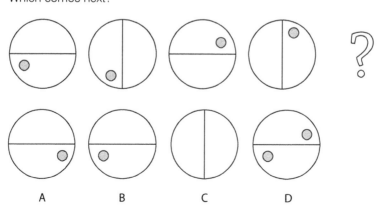

A   B   C   D

29   Which is the odd one out?

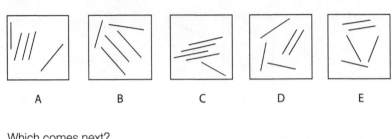

A   B   C   D   E

30   Which comes next?

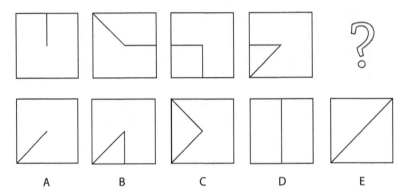

A   B   C   D   E

31   Which is the odd one out?

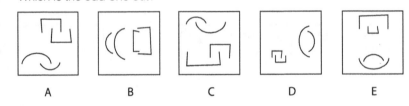

A   B   C   D   E

32   Which is the odd one out?

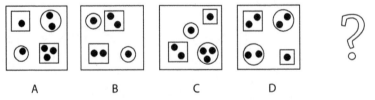

A   B   C   D

Answers

1 D	9 E	17 D	25 E
2 B	10 A	18 D	26 B
3 A	11 B	19 A	27 B
4 E	12 A	20 B	28 B
5 C	13 D	21 D	29 C
6 C	14 D	22 A	30 D
7 C	15 C	23 A	31 E
8 A	16 A	24 C	32 B

Scoring

Number right minus number wrong = _____

Plus 3 aged under 16, plus 1 if aged 17–20   + _____

Score on the test = _____

Use the following table to convert your test score to a score out of 10 or 'sten score'. You can then enter your 'sten score' in the chart on page 234.

Test score	1–2	3–4	5–6	7–9	10–12	13–15	16–18	19–21	22–25	26+
Sten score	1	2	3	4	5	6	7	8	9	10

Explanations

1   Only D has straight lines and corners.

2   The sequence is: square, circle, square, circle, square, thus B.

3   Only A has straight lines and corners.

4   The line across the square moves regularly in equal movements around the square so that the next movement will see the line from the top right to bottom left of the square, thus E.

5   Only C is not a 'regular' figure.

6   The square has to be seen with 'clock hands' in which one hand moves a quarter of an hour at a time and the other moves at an eighth of an hour, thus C.

7   Only C consists of two figures that are the same.

8   The small, shaded circle remains in the same position for two turns. It is

'shaded' in the third figure and also in the fourth figure where it must be at the bottom left. It will remain in the bottom left when the shade moves to the top of the square in the next figure.

9   E is the only figure to have two circles on the same side of the line. (There is nothing to choose between the oblique line of D and the horizontal line of E.)

10   There is a sequence – box, circle, triangle – so that the next large (outside) figure must be a circle. Each large figure next becomes an inside figure, but shaded. Thus in the third figure the shaded small box becomes the large shaded square and the next in turn will be the shaded small circle, which in the fifth figure will be large.

11   B is the only figure that has been 'turned over'.

12   There is a regular movement of a quarter turn.

13   In each of the figures, the line drawn across the figure connecting the corners is itself touched by a line that starts from a corner, except for D, where the line meets a side.

14   The circle has a horizontal line across it dividing the circle in half. A shaded half-circle moves a quarter turn around the circle so that it will next be at the left side of the circle.

15   C is the only figure not to contain a square.

16   The circle has a line dividing it vertically into two equal halves. A 'plate' or 'mask' exactly the size of half the circle revolves around the circle a quarter turn with each successive figure, thus – side left, bottom, side right, top and, next, side left.

17   D is the only figure to have both a shaded and a plain small figure on one side of the line.

18   The internal line or arm moves anti-clockwise.

19   The sum of the sides of the internal figure are more than the external figure in A.

20   The shaded space moves successively clockwise a quarter turn so will be on the right side in the figure that comes next. The white dot moves clockwise from corner to corner of the figure and is covered or masked by the black dot in the fourth figure, but will be at the bottom left hand side in the next figure. The black dot alternates between top left and bottom right corners and will be at the top left hand side in the next figure.

21   D is the only figure to have an odd number of items.

22   The smallest internal figure emerges to be the external figure for two turns whilst there is also a successive change from a complete shade to a plain or open drawing. Therefore, the next figure is a large, open square.

23   A has an internal figure whose sum of sides is more than the outside figure.

24   The shaded part moves from the top to the bottom of the figure. The white circle moves anti-clockwise to the corners of the figure, being masked by the shaded part in figures 3 and 4. In the next figure the shaded part will be at the bottom and the white circle in the top right hand corner.

25   E has a line emerging from two corners.

26   The shaded triangle moves a quarter turn anti-clockwise. The white triangle moves from top to bottom remaining in the same position for two turns and being covered by the shaded triangle when they are both in the same position.

27   B has more shaded circles than other signs, the others have the same number or less.

28   In the first figure the white 'mask' is at the top, then moves around a quarter of a turn with each successive figure, so that in the next figure it will be across the top once more, as in the first figure. The shaded circle stays in the same position on two turns, moving from bottom left of the circle in the first and second figures to top right in the third and fourth figures, so that it will be at bottom left again in the next figure, answer B. There is no reason for the answer to be D, because had there been two shaded circles these would have been revealed in the second figure and also because answer D does not show the 'mask' if a shaded circle is showing through it.

29   The lines in C are grouped as 4 and 1 as opposed to 3 and 2.

30   The figures show two lines moving, like clock hands, although one is moving one eighth of a turn anti-clockwise and one a quarter turn clockwise.

31   In E the two internal figures each have a smaller and larger component the smaller of which faces and fits in the compass of the larger figure.

32   B has six black dots whilst the others have seven.

Part Two
Abstract numerical tests

You are not expected to be proficient with arithmetic or mathematics in either of these tests. The numbers are only used as a device in which relationships are formed. Whilst it is necessary to know the basic rules of numbers – addition, subtraction, multiplication and division – only a minimal ability with these is required to grasp the larger, conceptual issues of how the numbers relate to each other. The aptitude being tested is the ability to assess the proportions of things, make comparative judgements and see how matters 'shape up' when other proportions are added or substituted. The process of thinking requires a balance of quantification, proportion and adjustment, checking and proving possibilities. Doing well in these tests may indicate a high level of mathematical potential, which is especially relevant to careers where evaluation of data and the determination of their significance are important.

Test 4, Reasoning, asks that you discover identical information in a different form from which the original is presented. You have to identify the essential elements that may find a correspondence elsewhere, then test and prove your assumptions. Establishing what is relevant and what can be discarded can find expression in careers in which expert comprehension of quantitative issues is valued, for example, senior financial and economic roles.

Test 5, Interpolation, is a similar way of investigating abstract, numerical potential. But where, in Test 4, the problem has to be approached 'from all sides', the problems in Interpolation are more obviously logical and sequential. You have to consider the proportions and relationships that are holding the problem together or the missing elements that will make the equation balance. Again, the potential for mathematics is assessed and where the result is higher than for verbal tests it is likely that suitable careers would have a numerical basis.

TEST 4

REASONING

Find out whether a pair of numbers matches any of the possible answer pairs. One of the pairs *sometimes* has a relationship with *one* of the four possible answers a), b), c) or d). You have to find the answer that matches one of the pairs. When none of the pairs matches any of the answers, tick e).

Example 1

1:2

a) 1:1   b) 2:1   c) 3:2   d) 3:7   e) none

Explanation of Example 1: for the pair you are given, one number is half the other number: 1 is half of 2; 2 is two times 1. The same relationship is true for answer b). It does not matter that the numbers are the other way round.

For the next example, look at the first pair, 4:2, and see if there is a relationship with any of the possible answer pairs. If not, look at the next pair, 9:3, to see if that pair has a relationship with any of the answer pairs. Possibly, neither has a relationship with any of the given answer pairs, in which case your answer would be e).

Example 2

4:2   9:3

a) 1:4   b) 2:7   c) 3:2   d) 1:3   e) none

Explanation of Example 2: the correct answer is d) because 1:3 goes with 9:3. With each, the larger figure is *three times* the smaller figure. The fact that the numbers are around the other way does not matter. Sometimes the numbers are the same way, sometimes they are not, and sometimes there is no relationship at all. None of the other possible answers fits with the other pair.

Example 3

4:16

a) 2:1   b) 3:7   c) 1:2   d) 4:1   e) none

Example 4

3:12   9:3

a) 4:5   b) 1:7   c) 1:5   d) 6:4   e) none

The answer to Example 3 is d) because 4:1 is the same relationship as 4:16. The answer to Example 4 is e) because none of the possible answers has a relationship with either of the possible pairs.

The test begins on the next page. Work as quickly and accurately as you can. You can do the items in any order you like, although the questions get increasingly difficult. Do not mark this book if it is not your own, but record your answers and any working out you need to do on separate paper. If you wish to gain an estimate of your aptitude, record the number of the question you are on after exactly 10 minutes. Otherwise, take as long as you wish to complete the items.

Timed test: 10 minutes

1   1:2
   a) 2:2   b) 6:1   c) 1:8   d) 1:2   e) none

2   1:3
   a) 3:1   b) 1:6   c) 2:1   d) 5:4   e) none

3   4:8
   a) 3:4   b) 8:4   c) 5:5   d) 3:3   e) none

4   6:3
   a) 3:2   b) 4:9   c) 5:4   d) 2:2   e) none

5   2:1
   a) 7:8   b) 1:1   c) 4:2   d) 6:5   e) none

6   2:3
   a) 1:3   b) 7:1   c) 4:6   d) 9:3   e) none

7   5:1
   a) 1:6   b) 1:10   c) 10:9   d) 15:3   e) none

8   14:7
   a) 12:10   b) 2:14   c) 8:3   d) 3:9   e) none

9   3:6 1:3
   a) 1:2   b) 4:1   c) 5:1   d) 3:3   e) none

10   1:1 3:3
   a) 1:6   b) 3:4   c) 2:9   d) 4:4   e) none

11   2:4 4:1
   a) 4:5   b) 3:3   c) 1:5   d) 7:3   e) none

12   3:2 2:8
   a) 1:5   b) 4:1   c) 9:1   d) 1:11   e) none

13   12:6 10:2
   a) 3:1   b) 5:1   c) 1:4   d) 4:1   e) none

14   26:13   15:3
a) 3:1   b) 1:6   c) 2:1   d) 5:4   e) none

15   16:8   24:8
a) 1:4   b) 3:4   c) 5:1   d) 1:3   e) none

16   4:20   9:18   6:36
a) 6:2   b) 4:5   c) 6:1   d) 2:20   e) none

17   15:3   6:24   5:10
a) 7:2   b) 3:1   c) 5:2   d) 6:1   e) none

18   100:50   27:9   32:8
a) 10:3   b) 5:1   c) 2:16   d) 9:3   e) none

19   12:2   13:2   4:8
a) 1:6   b) 1:4   c) 2:2   d) 1:3   e) none

20   24:3   15:6   4:28
a) 12:2   b) 14:2   c) 8:3   d) 3:10   e) none

21   3:4   9:3   1:3   8:4
a) 1:2   b) 1:4   c) 1:5   d) 6:10   e) none

22   9:3   5:23   4:21   2:24
a) 1:4   b) 5:3   c) 12:9   d) 12:2   e) none

23   9:5   6:4   13:8   15:9
a) 4:2   b) 3:1   c) 1:4   d) 3:7   e) none

24   6:20   30:7   23:3   22:2
a) 6:1   b) 1:4   c) 5:1   d) 3:33   e) none

25   15:9   24:20   7:35   11:10
a) 12:4   b) 8:64   c) 10:2   d) 1:1   e) none

26   100:10   11:111   7:70   35:7
a) 1:11   b) 5:1   c) 7:1   d) 10:11   e) none

27   4:6   9:5   14:2   16:14
a) 7:8   b) 12:6   c) 1:2   d) 7:6   e) none

28   16:3   24:5   44:10   36:3
a) 5:12   b) 11:4   c) 5:1   d) 12:1   e) none

29   100:11   8:88   27:3   128:16
a) 8:1   b) 10:1   c) 22:1   d) 32:2   e) none

30   51:6   126:18   38:3   28:4
a) 14.1   b) 24:8   c) 15:3   d) 17:2   e) none

31   14:3   19:6   11:32   17:26
a) 6:3   b) 7:3   c) 7:2   d) 3:4   e) none

32   13:12   10:9   9:8   8:11
a) 96:104   b) 60:52   c) 128:256   d) 48:45   e) none

33   3:5   4:3   7:4   9:5
a) 54:48   b) 16:20   c) 66:44   d) 28:16   e) none

34   512:128   444:333   99:297   153:68
a) 12:20   b) 63:21   c) 8:13   d) 17:11   e) none

35   13:11   39:55   66:26   52:99   165:110
a) 54:26   b) 14:4   c) 16:24   d) 15:12   e) none

36   17:8   19:13   21:20   39:43   29:19
a) 88:178   b) 4:7   c) 48:95   d) 95:145   e) none

Answers

1 d	7 d	13 b	19 a	25 c	31 e
2 a	8 e	14 c	20 b	26 b	32 a
3 b	9 a	15 d	21 a	27 a	33 d
4 e	10 d	16 c	22 e	28 d	34 b
5 c	11 e	17 e	23 e	29 a	35 c
6 c	12 b	18 d	24 d	30 d	36 d

Scoring

Number right minus number wrong = _____

Plus 3 aged under 16, plus 1 if aged 17–20   + _____

Score on the test = _____

Use the following table to convert your test score to a score out of 10 or 'sten score'. You can then enter your 'sten score' in the chart on page 234.

Test score	1–5	6–9	10–13	14–17	18–20	21–23	24–26	27–28	29–30	31+
Sten score	1	2	3	4	5	6	7	8	9	10

Explanations

1 1:2 = 1:2	10 1:1 = 4:4	19 12:2 = 1:6	28 36:3 = 12:1
2 1:3 = 3:1	11 none	20 4:28 = 14:2	29 128:16 = 8:1
3 4:8 = 8:4	12 2:8 = 4:1	21 8:4 = 1:2	30 51:16 = 17:2
4 none	13 10:2 = 5:1	22 none	31 none
5 2:1 = 4:2	14 26:13 = 2:1	23 none	32 13:12 = 96:104
6 2:3 = 4:6	15 24:8 = 1:3	24 22:2 = 3:33	33 7:4 = 28:16
7 5:1 = 15:3	16 6:36 = 6:1	25 7:35 = 10:2	34 99:297 = 63:21
8 none	17 none	26 35:7 = 5:1	35 165:110 = 16:24
9 3:6 = 1:2	18 27:9 = 9:3	27 16:14 = 7:8	36 29:19 = 95:145

TEST 5

INTERPOLATION

In this test you are given numbers that connect in some way. They connect along the row, but there is also a relationship with the numbers that are above or below each other. Sometimes a number is missing and a space mark, or line (–) has been put in its place. One of the numbers has been replaced by a question mark (?).

From the information given, you have to find the number that would replace the question mark.

Example 1

1	–	3	?
–	4	6	8

Answer [   ]

The most logical answer is 4, because it fits the sequence 1, 2, 3, 4 as a 2 could replace the space mark. Also, 4 is half of 8, in the same way that 3 is half of 6, 2 is half of 4, and 1 is half of 2. The answer, 4, makes all the numbers fit together logically:

1	2	3	4
2	4	6	8

Example 2

1	–	9	?
2	6	–	54

Answer [   ]

The numbers in the lower line are always twice the number in the row above. Also, from left to right, each number is multiplied three times.

1	3	9	27
2	6	18	54

Working out the correct numbers for the empty spaces can help you find the number that can replace the question mark. The test begins on the next page. Work as quickly and accurately as you can. You can do the items in any order you like, although the questions get increasingly difficult. Do not mark this book if it is not your own, but record your answers and any working out you need to do on separate paper. If you wish to gain an estimate of your aptitude, record the number of the question you are on after exactly 8 minutes. Otherwise, take as long as you wish to complete the items.

Timed test: 8 minutes

| **1** | 4 | 3 | 2 | ? | | | |
| | 4 | – | 2 | 1 | | *Answer* | |

| **2** | 2 | 4 | 6 | – | | | |
| | 4 | ? | 12 | 16 | | *Answer* | |

| **3** | 1 | ? | 5 | 7 | – | | |
| | – | 6 | – | – | 18 | *Answer* | |

| **4** | – | – | 8 | 4 | ? | | |
| | 64 | 32 | – | – | 4 | *Answer* | |

| **5** | 2 | 3 | ? | – | 13 | | |
| | – | – | 5 | 8 | 13 | *Answer* | |

| **6** | 3 | 6 | 9 | 12 | | | |
| | 9 | ? | – | 36 | | *Answer* | |

| **7** | 25 | 16 | 9 | 4 | | | |
| | – | 4 | ? | 2 | | *Answer* | |

| **8** | 3 | 7 | ? | – | | | |
| | 4 | 8 | 16 | 32 | | *Answer* | |

| **9** | 7 | 12 | 22 | – | 82 | | |
| | – | 4 | 9 | 19 | ? | *Answer* | |

| **10** | 13 | 14 | 16 | ? | 28 | | |
| | 1 | – | 4 | – | 16 | *Answer* | |

| **11** | 3 | 7 | 16 | 35 | ? | | |
| | 1 | 2 | 3 | – | 5 | *Answer* | |

| **12** | 11 | 14 | – | ? | | | |
| | 33 | 42 | 60 | 87 | | *Answer* | |

| **13** | 3 | 6 | 5 | 8 | 7 | – | |
| | 7 | 11 | 11 | 15 | 15 | ? | *Answer* |

14

?	5	7	12	–	
3	–	8	13	21	Answer

Answer [ ]

15

4	5	8	10	?	20	
10	8	20	16	40	–	Answer

Answer [ ]

16

3	7	5	?	7	11	
–	4	2	4	2	–	Answer

Answer [ ]

17

5	10	7	12	–	
10	30	?	60	54	Answer

Answer [ ]

18

6	13	20	–	34	
?	24	37	–	63	Answer

Answer [ ]

19

0	5	3	13	11	?	
5	–	10	2	20	–	Answer

Answer [ ]

20

13	?	22	31	53	
78	45	–	93	–	Answer

Answer [ ]

Answers

1 1	6 18	11 74	16 9
2 8	7 3	12 29	17 28
3 3	8 15	13 19	18 11
4 2	9 39	14 2	19 31
5 5	10 20	15 16	20 9

Scoring

Number right minus number wrong = _____

Plus 2 aged under 16, plus 1 if aged 17–20   + _____

Score on the test = _____

Use the following table to convert your test score to a score out of 10 or 'sten score'. You can then enter your 'sten score' in the chart on page 234.

Test score	1–2	3	4–5	6	7–8	9	10–12	13	14–15	16+
Sten score	1	2	3	4	5	6	7	8	9	10

Explanations

1   The numbers in the bottom line are the same as the numbers in the top line.

2   The numbers in the bottom line are twice the numbers in the top line.

3   The numbers in the top line ascend by 2. The numbers in the bottom line are twice the numbers in the top line.

4   The numbers in the top row are half those in the bottom row.

5   The numbers in both rows are the same. In each row each number is a sum of the two previous numbers.

6   The numbers in the bottom row are three times the numbers in the top row.

7   Each of the numbers in the top row is the number in the bottom row multiplied by itself (squared).

8   The number in the top row is 1 less than the number in the bottom row. The number in the top row can be found by adding the two previous numbers that are above and below each other.

9   The numbers in the top row are twice the previous number less 2. The numbers in the bottom line are twice the previous number plus 1. The numbers in both rows increase by 5, 10, 20, and so on.

10 In the top row the number of the difference between each number successively doubles. These differences are shown in the bottom line.

11 The numbers in the bottom line are an ascending series of which the missing number is 4. The numbers in the top line are twice the previous number in the line plus 1, plus 2, plus 3 and plus 4. The two lines of numbers have no obvious connection.

12 The number in the bottom line is three times the number above it. The number in the top line increases by 3, 6, 9, and so on.

13 The numbers in the top line are successively increased by 3 then reduced by 1. The numbers in the bottom line are successively double the number above plus 1 then double the number above and reduced by 1.

14 The numbers in the bottom line are the sum of the previous two numbers in the line. The numbers in the top line are 1 less than the numbers in the bottom line.

15 The numbers in the bottom line are successively minus 2, double the number and add 4, minus 4, double the number and add 4, minus 8. The bottom line numbers also double on every other occasion. The numbers in the top line are double the number add 2, double the number less 2, double the number add 4, double the number less 4, double the number add 8, double the number less 8. Also, on every other occasion, the number in the top line is half the number preceding it in the bottom line.

16 The difference between each pair of numbers in the top row gives the number to the right of that pair in the bottom row.

17 The number in the top line is multiplied by 2, 3, 4, 5 and 6 to produce the number in the bottom line.

18 The number in the bottom line is twice the number in the top line, less 1, less 2, less 3, and so on.

19 The top and bottom numbers of the first pair add to the top number of the second pair. This number, less 2, gives the top number of the second pair. The number 2 is the bottom number of the second pair. The pattern repeats so that the top and bottom numbers in the third pair are added to give the top number in the fourth pair. This is reduced by 2 to give the top number of the fifth pair. The number 2 is at the bottom of the fourth pair. The top and bottom numbers of the fifth pair are added to give the top number of the sixth pair.

20 The top number of each pair is multiplied successively by 6, 5, 4, 3 and 2 to give the bottom number so that the missing bottom numbers are 88 and 106.

Part Three
Abstract verbal tests

In the same way that the abstract numerical tests require some ability to count and to understand the rules of numbers, the abstract verbal tests require an understanding of what words mean and how sentences are formed to convey meaning. The vocabulary is not difficult, but forming accurate conclusions about what is being communicated becomes increasingly difficult as the tests proceed. The skill required lies in being able to evaluate information without being distracted by false information and without making assumptions about something that is not actually there. This type of verbal test is more likely to be confusing than any other type of test simply because words can have several meanings and all of us are sometimes taken in by distorted messages as well as those deliberately intended to deceive.

Tests 6 and 7 have a similar layout and are measuring essentially the same deductive potential. Be especially aware of the necessity of making logical conclusions from information that is given to you in an 'oblique way', that is, in a way that can be derived from other clues. Success on this test really does require a kind of aptitude that has much in common with detection. Test 6, Deduction, is a 'real' test that has been used by organizations to help discover executives with high-level reasoning skills. It is also very similar to the type of problems given to applicants for senior positions in public administration and for entry to business schools. Test 7, Analysis, is similarly demanding, but has been designed to be taken by younger people who may still be at school as well as by older people.

Success on these tests is a good indicator of 'academic' potential, particularly if you are good on the abstract numerical tests too. People who do well on these tests are generally good communicators in management or in other direct, face-to-face situations.

TEST 6

DEDUCTION

In this test you have to find the conclusion that follows from the information you are given. Sometimes there is information missing, but you will have enough to form a correct answer.

Read through the example below, which has been done for you. Before looking at the answers, try to work them out for yourself, ticking the answer to each question you think is correct. You will probably find it useful to have scrap paper available.

Example

Whilst Mr Black, Mr Saul and Mr Hardy travel to work by bus, Mr Jones and Mr Peters travel by train. Mr Black and Mr Saul also walk part of the way. Mr Saul, Mr Peters and Mr Hardy have season tickets.

1) Who has a season ticket, but also walks?

   a) Mr Black   b) Mr Saul   c) Mr Hardy
   d) Mr Jones   e) Mr Peters   f) cannot say

2) Who does not have a season ticket and does not walk?

   a) Mr Black   b) Mr Saul   c) Mr Hardy
   d) Mr Jones   e) Mr Peters   f) cannot say

3) Who travels by bus, but does not have a season ticket?

   a) Mr Black   b) Mr Saul   c) Mr Hardy
   d) Mr Jones   e) Mr Peters   f) cannot say

4)   How many people have neither a season ticket nor walk?

    a) one   b) two   c) three

    d) four   e) five   f) cannot say

5)   Who lives closest to a bus stop?

    a) Mr Black   b) Mr Saul   c) Mr Hardy

    d) Mr Jones   e) Mr Peters   f) cannot say

The answers are: 1) b, Mr Saul; 2) d, Mr Jones; 3) a, Mr Black; 4) a, one; 5) f, cannot say.

With problems of this type, it can be useful to lay out the information provided in the form of a table or diagram. This means that you do not have to 'carry' all the information in your head. Have spare paper available. The following is a possible way of laying out the information in the example problem:

Black	*Saul*	*Hardy*	*Jones*	*Peters*
bus	bus	bus	train	train
walk	walk			
	season	season		season

On the next page are several sets of information and you have to tick the correct answers. You can do the items in any order you like, although the questions get increasingly difficult. Do not mark this book if it is not your own, but record your answers and any working out you need to do on separate paper. If you wish to gain an estimate of your aptitude, record the number of the question you are on after exactly 20 minutes. Otherwise, take as long as you wish to complete the items.

Timed test: 20 minutes

A   Of three part-time employees, Mary Potter works longer hours than Fred Ruby, although Betty Simpson works longer hours than Mary Potter.

1   Who works the longest hours?

a) Mary Potter   b) Fred Ruby   c) Betty Simpson
d) cannot say

B   Frank and John use computers in their work. Gary, John and Frank are self-employed. Frank and Jack work part-time, whilst the others are all full-time. Jack and John are the only ones who work in insurance.

2   Who uses a computer to work full-time in insurance?

a) Frank   b) John   c) Jack
d) Gary   e) cannot say

3   Who does not work in insurance and does not have a computer?

a) Frank   b) John   c) Jack
d) Gary   e) cannot say

4   Who is the only one who is self-employed and works part-time?

a) Frank   b) John   c) Jack
d) Gary   e) cannot say

C   Different businesses occupy a three-storey building. The Architect is on the top floor, whilst the Estate Agent is on the floor below the Travel Agent. The Accountant is on the floor above the Publisher, as is the Estate Agent. The Travel Agent is on the same floor as the Car Rental Company. On the floor between the Publisher and the Car Rental Company is a Detective Agency.

5   Which business is on a floor by itself?

a) Architect   b) Estate Agent   c) Travel Agent
d) Accountant   e) Publisher   f) Car Rental
g) Detective Agency   h) cannot say

6   Which business occupies the largest floor space?

a) Architect   b) Estate Agent   c) Travel Agent
d) Accountant   e) Publisher   f) Car Rental
g) Detective Agency   h) cannot say

7 Of the options given, which businesses are on the same floor as the Accountant?

a) Architect   b) Estate Agent   c) Travel Agent
d) Accountant   e) Publisher   f) Car Rental
g) Detective Agency   h) cannot say

D   Sally, Cheryl, Laura, Tom and Sandy travel extensively on business. Four of them have visas for China. All, apart from Cheryl and Tom, have visas for Russia. Cheryl's only visa is for Pakistan, although only Sally and Sandy do not have a visa for Pakistan.

8 Who only has visas for China and Pakistan?

a) Sally   b) Cheryl   c) Laura
d) Tom   e) Sandy   f) cannot say

9 Who has the most visas?

a) Sally   b) Cheryl   c) Laura
d) Tom   e) Sandy   f) cannot say

10 Who travels most often?

a) Sally   b) Cheryl   c) Laura
d) Tom   e) Sandy   f) cannot say

11 Who are the two people who have identical visas?

a) Sally   b) Cheryl   c) Laura
d) Tom   e) Sandy   f) cannot say

12 How many visas do the group have between them?

a) 4   b) 5   c) 6
d) 7   e) 8   f) 9
g) 10   h) 11   i) 12
j) 13   k) 14   l) 15
m) 16   n) 17

13 Which is the most frequented country?

a) Pakistan   b) Russia   c) China
d) cannot say

E   Three athletes each receive a first, second and third prize for a different sporting event. Either Anne or Josie got the second prize for tennis. Anne got the same prize for throwing the javelin as Josie got for swimming. Tanya got the first prize for swimming, and her prize for the javelin was the same as Josie's for tennis and Anne's for swimming.

14 Who got the first prize for tennis?

a) Anne   b) Josie   c) Tanya
d) cannot say

15 Who was best with the javelin?

a) Anne   b) Josie   c) Tanya
d) cannot say

16 Who got the second prize for swimming?

a) Anne   b) Josie   c) Tanya
d) cannot say

F   Doppler's butterfly is only found in Asian countries, including India, Thailand, Japan, Malaysia and Cambodia, and in areas of non-forested South American countries, including Brazil, Argentina, Chile and Peru. It is very rare in Brazil, where it has black, elongated wings, whilst in Asia the wings are much shorter and coloured orange. In Chile they have only red wings, though these retain the characteristic South American shape.

17 In which country is the butterfly unlikely to have elongated wings?

a) Mexico   b) Chile   c) Argentina
d) Brazil   e) India   f) cannot say

18 Where is a forest-dwelling Doppler butterfly with orange wings most likely to be found?

a) Chile   b) Germany   c) Thailand
d) Australia   e) cannot say

19 Where is a desert-dwelling, elongated winged Doppler butterfly most likely to be found?

a) Thailand   b) India   c) Japan
d) Australia   e) Argentina   f) cannot say

20 Where is a purple Doppler butterfly most likely to be found?

a) France   b) India   c) Japan
d) Cambodia   e) Peru   f) cannot say

G To get to his home at Tranton Park, Geoff takes the 17.45 train from Central Station. Rona avoids public transport whenever possible, but walks with him to the station, where she has left her car. Her drive to her home in Hampton takes 15 minutes, although it would have taken exactly the same time by train. Like Geoff, Sam takes the train, but avoids the rush by taking the 17.15 from Central Station. Bella, who works in the same office as the rest and who prefers the train, always makes the journey with Sam as far as Hampton, where she lives. Sam continues to Nately, which is his home-town, a journey that is three times as long as hers. Geoff arrives at Tranton Park an hour and a quarter after Bella gets to Hampton.

21 Who probably has the longest journey?

a) Geoff   b) Rona   c) Sam
d) Bella   e) cannot say

22 Who is most likely to arrive home first?

a) Geoff   b) Rona   c) Sam
d) Bella   e) cannot say

23 Who, apart from Geoff, is most likely to travel by train?

a) Geoff   b) Rona   c) Sam
d) Bella   e) cannot say

24 Who never travels by train?

a) Geoff   b) Rona   c) Sam
d) Bella   e) cannot say

25 How many minutes is the journey time between Nately and Tranton Park?

a) 30   b) 15   c) 20
d) 10   e) 5   f) 45
g) cannot say

Answers

1 c	6 h	11 a/e	16 a	21 a
2 b	7 b/g	12 g	17 e	22 d
3 d	8 d	13 d	18 c	23 c/d
4 a	9 c	14 a	19 e	24 e
5 e	10 f	15 b	20 f	25 b

Scoring

Number right minus number wrong = _____

Plus 2 aged under 16, plus 1 if aged 17–20   + _____

Score on the test = _____

Use the following table to convert your test score to a score out of 10 or 'sten score'. You can then enter your 'sten score' in the chart on page 234.

Test score	1–6	7–8	9–10	11–12	13–14	15–16	17	18	19	20+
Sten score	1	2	3	4	5	6	7	8	9	10

Explanations

A   **1**   Mary longer than Fred
Betty longer than Mary
Therefore: Betty....Mary....Fred

B   **2, 3 and 4**

	Computers	Self-employed	Part-time	Full-time	Insurance
Frank	Y	Y	Y		
John	Y	Y		Y	Y
Gary		Y		Y	
Jack			Y		Y

C   **5, 6 and 7**

Top floor: Architect   (Note: Travel agent on floor above Estate Agent)

Accountant and Estate Agent   (So, as there are only three floors, above Publisher   the Estate Agent must be on the middle floor)

So: Top floor: <u>Architect</u>   <u>Travel Agent</u>
     Middle floor: <u>Estate Agent</u>   <u>Accountant</u>
     Lower floor: <u>Publisher</u>

Travel Agent and Car Rental Company are on the same floor

So: Top floor: <u>Architect</u>   <u>Travel Agent</u>   <u>Car Rental</u>
                    <u>Company</u>
     Middle floor: <u>Estate Agent</u>   <u>Accountant</u>
     Lower floor: <u>Publisher</u>

The Detective Agency is between the Publisher and the Car Rental Company (and we know that the Car Rental Company is on the top floor and the Publisher on the lower floor)

So: Top floor: <u>Architect</u>   <u>Travel Agent</u>   <u>Car Rental</u>
                    <u>Company</u>
     Middle floor: <u>Estate Agent</u>   <u>Accountant</u>   <u>Detective Agency</u>
     Lower floor: <u>Publisher</u>

D   8, 9, 10, 11, 12, and 13

	China	Russia	Pakistan
Sally	Y	Y	
Cheryl			Y
Laura	Y	Y	Y
Tom	Y		Y
Sandy	Y	Y	

- As Cheryl only has a visa for Pakistan, it must be the other four who have visas for China.

E   14, 15 and 16

Tanya got the first prize for swimming:

	Swimming	Tennis	Javelin
Anne			
Josie			
Tanya	1st		

Tanya's prize for the javelin was the same as Josie's for tennis and Anne's for swimming, so this must be a 2nd or 3rd prize. And either Anne or Josie had got the second prize for tennis. Josie and Anne both had second prizes for either swimming or tennis. So only Tanya could have got the 3rd prize for tennis:

	Swimming	Tennis	Javelin
Anne			
Josie			
Tanya	1st	3rd	

Tanya therefore got the second prize for the javelin. And her prize for the javelin was the same as Josie got for tennis and Anne's for swimming:

	Swimming	Tennis	Javelin
Anne	2nd		
Josie		2nd	
Tanya	1st	3rd	2nd

Therefore, Josie must have got third place for swimming and the remaining empty spaces in the chart can be completed:

	Swimming	Tennis	Javelin
Anne	2nd	1st	3rd
Josie	3rd	2nd	1st
Tanya	1st	3rd	2nd

F   17, 18, 19 and 20

		Population	Wing colour	Wing length
Asia				
	India		Orange	Shorter
	Thailand		Orange	Shorter
	Japan		Orange	Shorter
	Malaysia		Orange	Shorter
	Cambodia		Orange	Shorter
S. America				
(non-forest)	Brazil	Rare	Black	Elongated
	Argentina			Elongated
	Chile		Red	Elongated
	Peru			Elongated

G   21, 22, 23, 24 and 25

	17.15 Train	Walks	17.15 Car	17.45 Train	Time to Hampton	Time to Nately	Time to Tranton
Geoff		Y		Y			60 mins*
Rona		Y	Y		15 mins		
Sam	Y					45 mins*	
Bella	Y				15 mins		

*Sam's journey is three times as long as Bella's. Geoff arrives home an hour and a quarter after Bella who caught a train half an hour earlier than him.

TEST 7

ANALYSIS

This test looks at how well you can draw logical conclusions from the information you have been given. There is always sufficient information for you to work out the correct answer. You should not draw upon any previous experience or information you suppose might be relevant. You are given some facts and some possible answers. Tick the letter which corresponds with the correct answer.

Example 1

The town of Newport is further west than the town of Flatpeak, although not so far west as the town of Daybridge.

Which town is furthest east?

Answers: a) Newport   b) Daybridge   c) Flatpeak

The answer cannot be a) because Newport is west of Flatpeak. It cannot be b) because Daybridge is even further west, so Flatpeak must be to the east of Daybridge. The answer is c).

Example 2

Fred, Mack and John all have two different cars each. One of them does not have a Ford. Mack is the only one to have a Ferrari. John has a Ford. Fred and Mack have Buicks.

Who has a Rolls-Royce?

Answers: a) Fred   b) Mack   c) John

The answer is c). It cannot be a), because Fred has a Ford and a Buick. It cannot be b), because Mack has a Ferrari and a Buick.

Because of the amount of information you are sometimes asked to deal with, it is recommended that you have a piece of scrap paper so that you can, if you wish, make notes or plans. Tables like the following are often helpful.

	PEOPLE		
CARS	Fred	Mack	John
Ferrari			
Ford			
Buick			
Rolls-Royce			

You should have scrap paper and pencil ready in case you need them. Do not mark this book if it is not your own, but record your answers and any working out you need to do on separate paper. If you wish to gain an estimate of your aptitude, record the number of the question you are on after exactly 15 minutes. Otherwise, take as long as you wish to complete the items.

Timed test: 15 minutes

A   Emma lives further up the hill than Jane. Pauline lives further up the hill than Emma.

1   Who lives furthest up the hill?

a) Emma   b) Jane   c) Pauline

B   All the girls like sport. Sue and Josie like tennis, while Sally and Anne like running. Both Sue and Anne like swimming.

2   Who likes tennis and swimming?

a) Sue   b) Josie   c) Sally   d) Anne

3   Who likes swimming and running?

a) Sue   b) Josie   c) Sally   d) Anne

C   Mr Everton and Mr Soames have longer holidays than Mr Francke. Mr Porter has a shorter holiday than Mr Francke, whilst Mr Peters has a longer holiday than Mr Francke.

4   Who has the shortest holiday?

a) Mr Everton   b) Mr Soames   c) Mr Francke
d) Mr Porter   e) Mr Peters

D   Toby, Rob and Frank all take a holiday by the sea, whilst Sam, Jo and Tony go hiking in the mountains. Frank, Sam and Jo travel by air. Jo, Rob and Tony do not enjoy their holiday.

5   Who goes to the sea and does not enjoy the holiday?

a) Toby   b) Rob   c) Frank
d) Sam   e) Jo   f) Tony

6   Who does not travel by air and goes hiking?

a) Toby   b) Rob   c) Frank
d) Sam   e) Jo   f) Tony

E   In reverse order, the most popular holiday tours offered by a travel company are Toronto, Florida, Rome and Paris, although Rome is extremely popular whatever the time of year. After a marketing promotion, Toronto becomes more popular than Rome, but less popular than Florida.

7   Which tour is most popular after the marketing promotion?

a) Toronto   b) Florida   c) Rome   d) Paris

8   Which tour is least popular after the marketing promotion?

a) Toronto   b) Rome   c) Florida   d) Paris

F   Fred, John, Garth and Joe all have children. Fred and John are the only two to have boys. John and Joe take their children to school by bus, whilst it is near enough to school for the others to walk. Fred and Joe are car owners, and sometimes do use their cars to get the children to school.

9 Who owns a car, but usually goes to the school by bus?

a) Fred   b) Joe   c) John   d) Garth

10 Who does not own a car and has a daughter?

a) Fred   b) Joe   c) John   d) Garth

G   In a museum, Modern Sculpture is to be found on the floor below Watercolours. Greek Pottery is on the floor above the Oil Paintings. The top floor contains the Italian Collection. Watercolours are on the same floor as South American Art, whereas the Oil Paintings are on the floor below Modern Sculpture.

11 What is to be found on the lowest floor?

a) Modern Sculpture   b) Watercolours   c) Greek Pottery
d) Oil Paintings   e) Italian Collection   f) South American Art

12 Which two are on the same floor?

a) Modern Sculpture and Greek Pottery

b) Watercolours and Oil Paintings

c) Oil Paintings and South American Art

d) none of these

H   Casey, Stuart, Ritchie, Billie and Colin all buy their own vehicles. Casey and Colin have room for three passengers as well as themselves. The others only have room for one passenger besides themselves. Ritchie and Casey have good front tyres, though the other tyres on all of the other vehicles are dangerous. Casey and Billie have vehicles that use diesel fuel. The others have vehicles that use petrol.

13 Who can take three passengers in their diesel vehicle?

a) Casey   b) Stuart   c) Ritchie
d) Billie   e) Colin

14 How many people have dangerous tyres on diesel vehicles that only have room for one passenger?

a) 5   b) 4   c) 3
d) 2   e) 1   f) none

15 Who can only take one passenger, but has good tyres?

a) Casey   b) Stuart   c) Ritchie
d) Billie   e) Colin

I   Mrs Booth has difficulty feeding her four children as each one will only eat certain foods. Sharon and Robina will eat rice and lamb. Kelly and Sharon are the only ones who like bread and cheese. Kelly and Sam both eat chicken and bread.

16 Which is the only food that Sharon does not eat?

a) bread   b) chicken   c) lamb
d) rice   e) cheese

17 Who eats cheese, chicken and bread?

a) Sharon   b) Kelly   c) Robina
d) Sam

18 Who does not eat cheese, but does eat lamb and rice?

a) Sharon   b) Kelly   c) Robina
d) Sam

19 Which food will be acceptable to most of the children?

a) bread   b) rice   c) lamb
d) cheese   e) chicken

J   Mr Marx's and Mr Bagshaw's cars are black. The others have red ones. Mr Bagshaw and Mrs Chance have a white stripe on the sides of their cars. Miss Jenkins has a blue stripe on the side of her car. Mr Fleming and Mr Marx have silver stripes on the sides of their cars. Miss Jenkins's and Mr Fleming's have blue upholstery, the others have white.

20 Who has a car with blue upholstery and a silver stripe?

a) Mr Bagshaw   b) Miss Jenkins   c) Mrs Chance
d) Mr Fleming   e) Mr Marx

21 Who has a car with a silver stripe and white upholstery?

a) Mr Bagshaw   b) Miss Jenkins   c) Mrs Chance
d) Mr Fleming   e) Mr Marx

22 Who has the red car with a blue stripe and matching upholstery?

a) Mr Bagshaw   b) Miss Jenkins   c) Mrs Chance
d) Mr Fleming   e) Mr Marx

K   In a 'knockout' basketball competition, Centurions are beaten by Raiders. Saracens beat Centurions. Saracens are beaten by Raiders and Aztecs. Centurions and Raiders are beaten by Aztecs.

23 How many games do Saracens win?

a) 1   b) 2   c) 3
d) 4   e) 0

24 How many games do Raiders win?

a) 1   b) 2   c) 3
d) 4   e) 0

25 Who emerge as the champions?

a) Raiders   b) Saracens   c) Aztecs
d) Centurions

L   Stopping at the shop on the way to school, Cheryl and Tom are the only ones not to buy chocolate. Of the five children, four of them, including Laura, buy fudge. Unlike the others, Sally, Cheryl and Sandy do not buy any toffee. In fact, Cheryl only buys fruit gums as she does not like other kinds of sweets.

26 Who only had a piece of toffee and a piece of fudge?

a) Sally   b) Cheryl   c) Laura
d) Tom   e) Sandy

27 Who had three sweets?

a) Sally   b) Cheryl   c) Laura
d) Tom   e) Sandy

28 Who are the two people who took the same number and type of sweets?

a) Sally and Laura   b) Sandy and Laura   c) Laura and Tom
d) Tom and Sandy   e) Sandy and Sally

29 In total, how many sweets were taken by the group?

a) 7   b) 8   c) 9
d) 10   e) 11   f) 12

M   Jane, Rachel and Tessa are girls who are wearing a jacket, coat or skirt in blue, green or red. None of these articles of clothing is the same colour and each girl is wearing a different colour. The coat belonging to Tessa is not green. Rachel's jacket and Jane's skirt are the same colour. Tessa's skirt is red. Her jacket, Rachel's skirt and Jane's coat are all the same colour.

30 What colour is Tessa's coat?

a) blue   b) green   c) red

31 What colour is Jane's jacket?

a) blue   b) green   c) red

32 Which girl has the green coat?

a) Jane   b) Rachel   c) Tessa

33 Which girl has the blue jacket?

a) Jane   b) Rachel   c) Tessa

Answers

1 c	7 d	13 a	19 a	25 c	31 c
2 a	8 b	14 e	20 d	26 d	32 a
3 d	9 b	15 c	21 e	27 c	33 b
4 d	10 d	16 b	22 b	28 e	
5 b	11 d	17 b	23 a	29 d	
6 f	12 a	18 c	24 b	30 a	

Scoring

Number right minus number wrong = _____

Plus 4 aged under 16, plus 2 if aged 17–20   + _____

Score on the test = _____

Use the following table to convert your test score to a score out of 10 or 'sten score'. You can then enter your 'sten score' in the chart on page 234.

Test score	1–4	5–6	7–8	9–10	11–13	14–19	20–23	24–27	28–29	30+
Sten score	1	2	3	4	5	6	7	8	9	10

Explanations

A   1   Emma is further up than Jane   Pauline is further up than Emma

So:

Pauline
Emma
Jane

B   2 and 3

	Sue	Josie	Sally	Anne
Tennis	Y	Y		
Running			Y	Y
Swimming	Y			Y

C   4

	Francke	shorter than	Everton/Soames
Porter shorter than	Francke		
	Francke	shorter than	Peters

D   5 and 6

	Sea	Hiking	Air	Do not enjoy
Toby	Y			
Rob	Y			Y
Frank	Y		Y	
Sam		Y	Y	
Jo		Y	Y	Y
Tony		Y		Y

E   7 and 8

Before, least popular: Toronto   Florida   Rome   Paris   most popular

After, least popular: Rome   Toronto   Florida Paris   most popular

F   9 and 10

	Fred	Joe	John	Garth
Boys	Y		Y	
Girls		Y		Y
Bus		Y	Y	
Near to walk	Y			Y
Own car	Y	Y		
Sometimes use car	Y	Y		

G   11 and 12   The separate facts are as follows:

Watercolours	Greek Pottery	TOP FLOOR Italian Collection	Watercolours/South American Art	Modern Sculpture
Modern Sculpture	Oil Paintings			Oil Paintings

So:

Watercolours/South American Art
Modern Sculpture/Greek Pottery
Oil Paintings

N.B. It is not necessary to know where the Italian Collection is in order to answer the questions.

H   13, 14 and 15

	Casey	Stuart	Ritchie	Billie	Colin
3 passengers	Y				Y
1 passenger		Y	Y	Y	
Good front tyres	Y		Y		
Dangerous tyres		Y		Y	Y
Diesel	Y			Y	
Petrol		Y	Y		Y

I   16, 17, 18 and 19

	Sharon	Kelly	Robina	Sam
Rice	Y		Y	
Lamb	Y		Y	
Bread	Y	Y		Y
Cheese	Y	Y		
Chicken		Y		Y

J   20, 21 and 22

	Marx	Bagshaw	Chance	Jenkins	Fleming
Black car	Y	Y			
Red car			Y	Y	Y
White stripe		Y	Y		
Blue stripe				Y	
Silver stripe	Y				Y
Blue upholstery				Y	Y
White upholstery	Y	Y	Y		

K   23, 24 and 25

(Winners on top line)	Raiders	Saracens	Aztecs	Centurions
Raiders			win	
Saracens	win		win	
Aztecs				
Centurions	win	win	win	

L   26, 27, 28 and 29

	Sally	Cheryl	Laura	Tom	Sandy
Chocolate	Y		Y		Y
Fudge	(Y)		Y	(Y)	(Y)
Toffee			Y	Y	
Fruit gums		Y			

N.B. (Y) is established as four children bought fudge and one of them could not be Cheryl as she only bought fruit gums.

M   30, 31, 32 and 33

	Jane	Rachel	Tessa
Jacket		X	Y
Coat	Y		Not green
Skirt	X	Y	Red

X shows that Rachel's jacket and Jane's skirt are the same colour. Y shows that Tessa's jacket, Rachel's skirt and Jane's coat are the same colour. As Tessa's coat is not green, it must be blue, which makes her jacket, Rachel's skirt and Jane's coat green:

	Jane	Rachel	Tessa
Jacket		X	Green
Coat	Green		Blue
Skirt	X	Green	Red

As Jane already has a green and red item, her skirt must be blue, which must be the same colour as Rachel's jacket. Both Jane and Rachel now both have blue and green items, so Jane's jacket and Rachel's coat must be red:

	Jane	Rachel	Tessa
Jacket	Red	Blue	Green
Coat	Green	Red	Blue
Skirt	Blue	Green	Red

Part Four

Physical tests

The tests in this section are representative of a type that have been used with great success by occupational psychologists. Over many years organizations have sought people with a natural aptitude for understanding the cause and effect of physical forces, so that these can be acted upon in concrete ways. These tests give evidence of the potential to apply intelligence to make things happen. Although talent in both areas may be realized in all sorts of practical ways, the long-term career path will also depend upon the strength of your other visual and numerical skills, which can complement and extend your potential further.

Test 8, Dynamics, presents mechanical problems as well as others connected with forces. It may at first glance seem strange, but relatively little in the way of past experience is required if you have the underlying aptitude to solve these problems. This is why the test has been particularly useful in identifying people for engineering and related disciplines, especially among women whose education may have disadvantaged them in relation to men, who were, historically, more likely to have been exposed to mechanics.

Test 9, Tracing, requires an aptitude to trace through a pattern without deviating from the core of the problem. An important element is the ability to maintain focus and control. If you do better on this test than Test 8 you are more likely to be drawn to the more schematic areas of engineering and planning connected with electrics, electronics, diagrams and computer hardware.

TEST 8

DYNAMICS

This tests your understanding of how things work. There is a written question and a drawing. Together, they contain all the information you need to answer the question.

Example

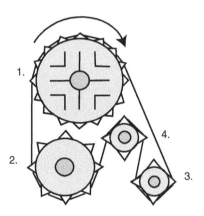

A chain is passed around four wheels, 1, 2, 3 and 4, so that the large wheel, 1, moves clockwise. Which of the wheels turns anti-clockwise?

a) 1   b) 2   c) 3   d) 4   e) none

The answer is 4.

You can do the items in any order you like. Do not mark this book if it is not your own, but record your answers and any working out you need to do on separate paper. If you wish to gain an estimate of your aptitude, record the number of the question you are on after exactly 10 minutes. Otherwise, take as long as you wish to complete the items.

Timed test: 10 minutes

1   Which ball is heaviest?

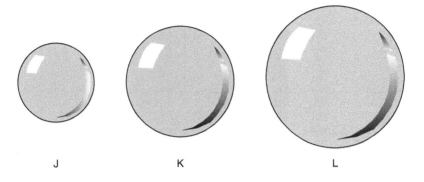

J   K   L

a) All weigh the same   b) L is heaviest   c) cannot say   d) J is heaviest

2   Three rubber wheels, A, B and C are touching so that if one moves the others must also move. If wheel A turns clockwise, which way will wheel C turn?

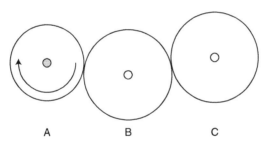

A   B   C

a) anti-clockwise   b) all the same way   c) clockwise   d) none will turn

3   A section through a dam is shown. At which point is the dam strongest?

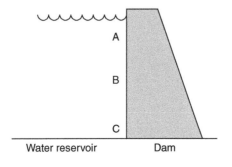

Water reservoir   Dam

a) At point A   b) At point B   c) At point C   d) All equally

4   In the same dam, at which point is the water coldest?

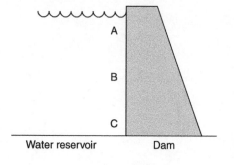

Water reservoir   Dam

a) At point A   b) At point B   c) At point C   d) All equally

5   The beam is twice as thick at one end as the other. At what point can it be placed on the wall, and at a right angle to the wall, so that it balances?

4 × 4

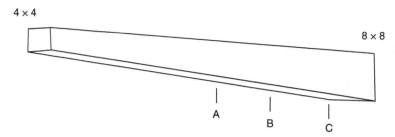

8 × 8

A   B   C

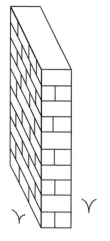

a) point A   b) point B   c) point C   d) needs support at both ends

6   When rays of light hit a lens, in which direction do they continue?

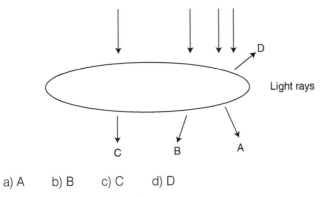

Light rays

a) A   b) B   c) C   d) D

7   A band passes around all the wheels so that they can all be turned by the driving wheel. When the driving wheel turns clockwise, which way does wheel W turn?

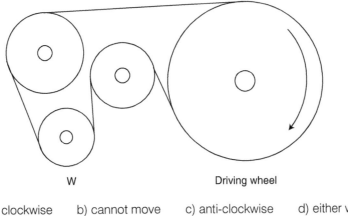

W   Driving wheel

a) clockwise   b) cannot move   c) anti-clockwise   d) either way

8   The drawing shows a cross-section of a wall, with a shelf upright against it. By means of a hinge, the shelf can be folded upright against the wall. It can be let down to the horizontal, being held at point H by a rope, which is suspended from a hook, A, B or C. When the shelf is let down and supported by the rope, which hook is least likely to be pulled out of the wall?

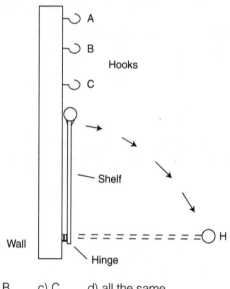

a) A   b) B   c) C   d) all the same

9   If the three iron bars are all the same length, which one will support the greatest weight?

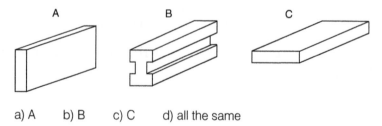

a) A   b) B   c) C   d) all the same

10   Three racing cars travel at equal speed round the built-up curve of a bend. Which car is most likely to slip?

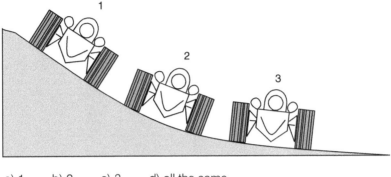

a) 1   b) 2   c) 3   d) all the same

11   If three racing cars are level with each other, side by side as they go into the bend, and all are also level as they come out of the bend, which car is travelling fastest?

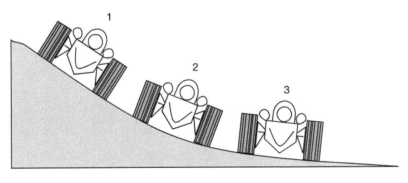

a) 1   b) 2   c) 3   d) all the same

12 This old-fashioned 'grandfather clock' pendulum and weight are made of iron. To keep correct time, in which direction might the weight need to be adjusted in summer?

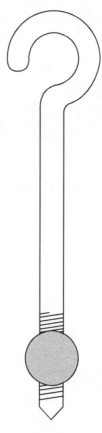

a) upwards   b) will not need adjustment   c) downwards

13   To lever up the large, heavy weight with the least effort, by pushing down in the direction of the arrow, at which point under the beam should the block be placed?

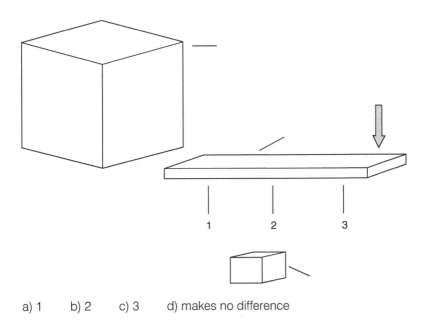

a) 1   b) 2   c) 3   d) makes no difference

14   A heavy metal bar is fixed inside a cardboard tube. When the tube is placed on a slope, as shown, which direction will the tube roll?

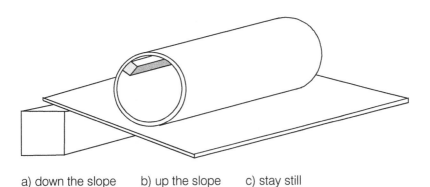

a) down the slope   b) up the slope   c) stay still

15   When the driving wheel 1 turns in the direction shown, wheel 2 turns…

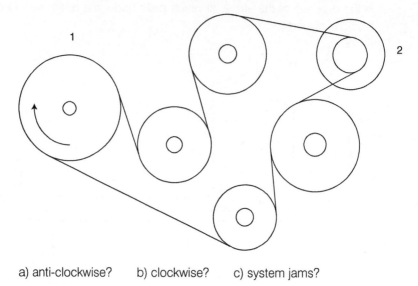

a) anti-clockwise?   b) clockwise?   c) system jams?

16   Assuming that the belt and wheels did not jam, which wheel would turn fastest?

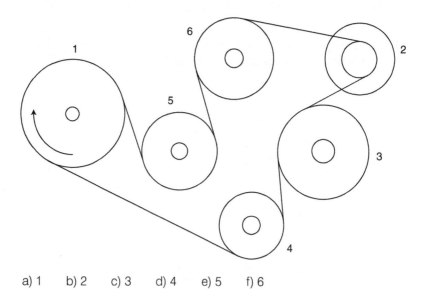

a) 1   b) 2   c) 3   d) 4   e) 5   f) 6

17 Two cars, A and B, one travelling from the north, N, due south, S, and the other from the west, W, due east, E, collide at point P. They come to rest in the region of south east, as shown. If the slower car was travelling exactly at the speed limit, which car was probably breaking the speed limit?

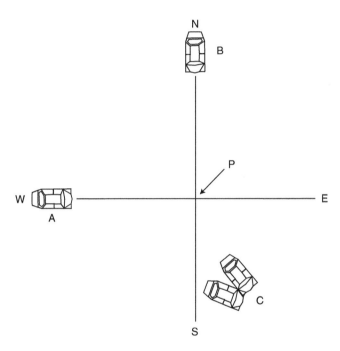

a) A   b) B   c) cannot tell

18 The ladders, 1 and 2, and the walls are viewed from the side. Which ladder is safer when climbed?

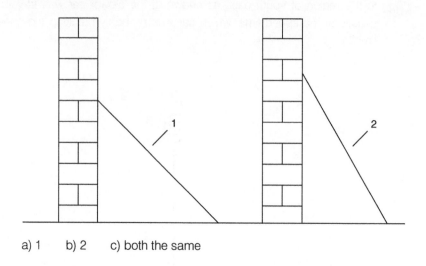

a) 1   b) 2   c) both the same

19 In a hot-water cylinder, from which outlet should hot water be taken?

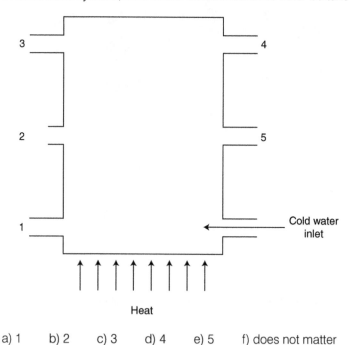

a) 1   b) 2   c) 3   d) 4   e) 5   f) does not matter

20 When the spacecraft is not affected by the Earth's gravity, and the thrust of the rocket is zero, the astronaut will:

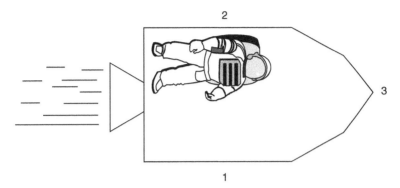

a) fall to side 1
b) stay where he is at side 2
c) be thrust towards the nose at 3

21 In space, when the stationary vehicle accelerates, the spaceman will:

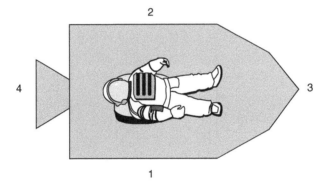

a) be thrust towards the nose at 3
b) fall down towards side 1
c) float upwards, due to weightlessness, towards 2
d) fall on his head on the floor at side 4

22   When wheel 1 turns clockwise, which way does wheel 4 turn?

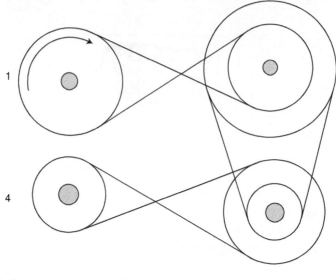

a) clockwise   b) anti-clockwise   c) system jams

23   In which direction does a steel ball continue after impact on a rigid, heavy steel block?

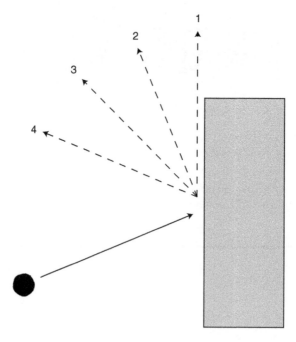

a) 1   b) 2   c) 3   d) 4

24 In which direction will ball 3 move when ball 1 is struck as shown?

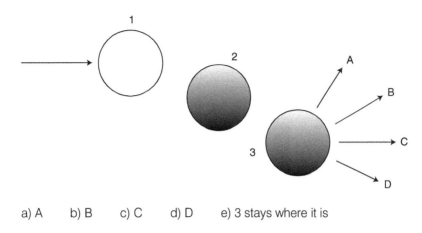

a) A   b) B   c) C   d) D   e) 3 stays where it is

25 Which way will helical gear H turn when helical gear M turns as shown?

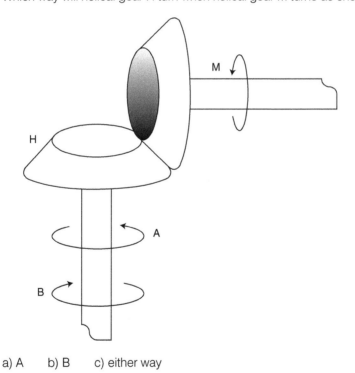

a) A   b) B   c) either way

Answers

1 c	6 a	11 a	16 b	21 d
2 c	7 a	12 a	17 b	22 a
3 c	8 a	13 a	18 b	23 d
4 c	9 b	14 b	19 c	24 c
5 b	10 c	15 b	20 b	25 b

Scoring

Number right minus number wrong = _____

Plus 2 aged under 16, plus 1 if aged 17–20   + _____

Score on the test = _____

Use the following table to convert your test score to a score out of 10 or 'sten score'. You can then enter your 'sten score' in the chart on page 234.

Test score	1–5	6–7	8–9	10–11	12–13	14–15	16–17	18–19	20–21	22+
Sten score	1	2	3	4	5	6	7	8	9	10

Explanations

1   Weight cannot necessarily be deduced from size.
2   A causes B to move anti-clockwise, which in turn causes C to rotate clockwise.
3   The dam must be strongest at C where it is withstanding the greatest pressure.
4   At C as temperature decreases with depth.
5   Although A is the middle of the beam, it will be heavier on one side. Relative volumes and their weights seem best balanced at B.
6   As rays of light hit the surface they will be turned to move through the lens at an angle 90 degrees to the surface, roughly in the direction indicated by arrow B. However, when the light moving through the lens hits the outer surface it will emerge at an angle 90 degrees to the surface of the lens, roughly in the direction of arrow A.
7   The wheels all turn clockwise apart from the wheel in the middle where the band passes in a contra direction.

8   Hooking at A gives the slightest angle between the rope and the wall so that, because the 'pull' of the rope is more downwards rather than outwards at A than it would be at B or C, A is least likely to be pulled out.

9   Although having less height than A or width than C, the section of B has the greater overall surface and its section is least likely to bend or twist either vertically or horizontally.

10 If they entered the curve at the same speed, car 3 would emerge at the end of the curve in front of 2, which would be in front of 1, because car 3 travels the shortest distance. It is therefore most likely to slip on the bend especially as it receives least corresponding pressure from the bank.

11 Car 1 has travelled furthest and therefore fastest.

12 The effect of heat upon iron is to make it expand so that the pendulum will swing more slowly in summer, so that the weight will need to be moved upwards during the summer to maintain regularity of beat.

13 Greatest leverage will be obtained by placing the block at point 1.

14 The weight of the bar acting in a vertically downward direction will make the tube roll up the slope.

15 The band moves around the surface of 2 in the same direction as 1.

16 Wheel 2 turns fastest as it is the smallest circle (or cog) around which the band passes.

17 The cars have been pushed further south than east so that car B must have had the greater force or speed.

18 As the base of the ladder moves away from the vertical the less any weight is pushed safely into the ground.

19 Hot water rises so that hot water is best drawn from the top of the cylinder. 3 is a marginally better answer than 4 because this would ensure the best flow of water through the cylinder.

20 Without any gravitational forces the astronaut continues in the same position and at the same speed as the craft.

21 Upon acceleration, it is only the craft that moves, whilst the spaceman will only begin to move when he encounters and is then propelled by the floor of the craft.

22 After wheel 1, the second wheel turns in the opposite direction, because the band connecting the two wheels has been crossed. The third wheel moves in the same direction as wheel 2, because the bands go the same way around both wheels. As the bands are crossed between wheels 3 and 4, wheel 4 will turn in the opposite direction to wheel 3, therefore clockwise.

23 As both items are steel and the block is rigid, the direction of the ball is likely to be almost equal and opposite to the direction of its impact, therefore 4.

24 Ball 1 will strike ball 2 driving it at an angle of about 45 degrees to hit ball 3 at approximately the same angle making an angle of 90 degrees so that ball 3 continues horizontally in the same direction as the first ball.

25 Gear M causes H to move in a contrary direction to itself so that, if in the diagram M is rotating clockwise H will rotate anti-clockwise as B

TEST 9

TRACING

In this test, you have to follow a line from the left-hand side of the page until you arrive at the right-hand side. Each line goes straight across other lines it comes to. Sometimes the line returns across the page before ending on the right-hand side. Where the line ends is a small picture or symbol.

Your task is to locate the symbol in the chart and see what letter is underneath it. Then, you tick the box underneath that letter where the line first started on the left-hand side of the page. In the example below, you can see the chart with pictures and letters. A letter goes with each picture.

On the left-hand side of the page are boxes underneath letters where you have to place your tick. If you start with the first box and follow the line along, you will see that it comes out at a picture of a heart. In the chart, underneath the heart, is the letter 'd'. So, 'd' has been ticked in the box where the line started. Try the other lines yourself.

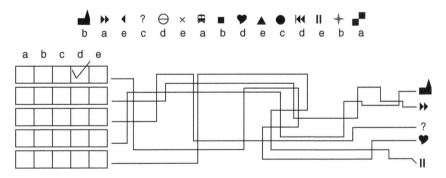

The first of the examples was done for you – the answer was 'd'. The answer to the next is 'a', then 'c', then 'b' and 'e'.

The test on the next page is done in just the same way. Work as quickly as you can. If this is not your book record your answers on a separate sheet of paper.

Timed test: 5 minutes

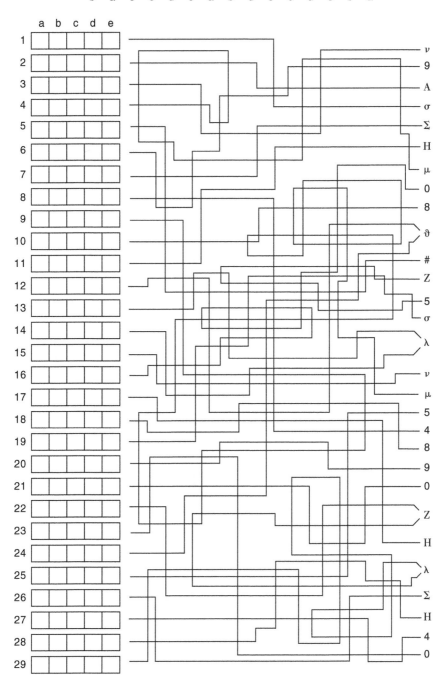

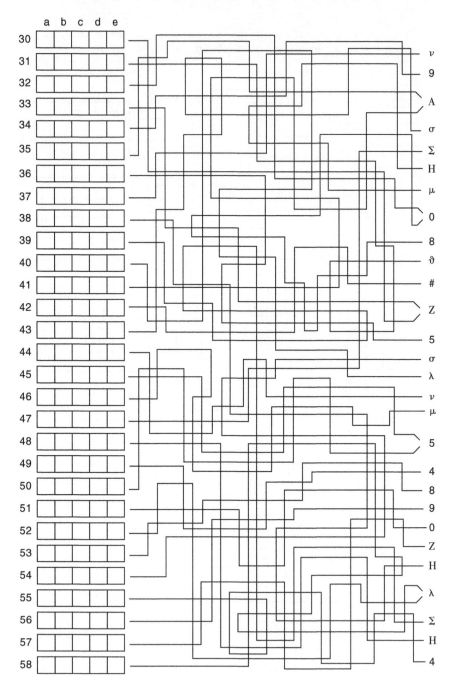

Answers

1 d	11 c	21 a	31 d	41 a	51 a
2 a	12 d	22 a	32 a	42 e	52 e
3 c	13 e	23 a	33 a	43 d	53 b
4 d	14 e	24 d	34 b	44 c	54 d
5 e	15 c	25 b	35 a	45 b	55 e
6 b	16 a	26 e	36 b	46 d	56 b
7 e	17 c	27 e	37 c	47 e	57 a
8 e	18 b	28 c	38 c	48 c	58 e
9 d	19 d	29 e	39 e	49 e	
10 b	20 b	30 a	40 e	50 b	

Scoring

Number right minus number wrong =   _____

Plus 2 if aged under 16   + _____

Score on the test =   _____

Use the following table to convert your test score to a score out of 10 or 'sten score'. You can then enter your 'sten score' in the chart on page 234.

Test score	1–20	21–23	24–26	27–29	30–32	33–35	36–38	39–41	42–44	45+
Sten score	1	2	3	4	5	6	7	8	9	10

Part Five
Spatial tests

The tests in this section require you to 'see' an object in your mind. Not only that, but to 'move' the object in your mind, so that you can see what it looks like from behind and also when it is upside down. Being able to recognize shapes and their dimensions is a talent that can have all manner of imaginative visual applications. In psychological terms it can often point to flexibility of thought and, of course, artistic creativity. The ability to accurately discriminate among rotating and changing shapes in some way replicates how many people 'turn things over in their mind'. Original possibilities and outcomes often arise from this process. If you do well on this test you may well be the type of person who thinks laterally or 'out of the box'.

Test 10, Formation, asks you to choose between different abstract shapes, the purpose being to assess your talent for judging the orientation of lines, contours and forms. Potential here may be expressed in some artistic form, literally in art and design, but, depending upon other talents that may emerge on the other tests, could be applied to areas of technology or geography, if you are numerically minded as well, or to writing or media work, if your strength is also on the verbal side.

Test 11, 3D tests, makes similar demands as the test of Formation, but the shapes themselves are regular and retain their dimensions. They do not demand the same 'flow' as the test of Formation, but do ask for a structured approach to the solution of the problem that has more in common with tasks associated with planning, architecture and with all sorts of design work. Again, unlike the Formation test, the specifically three-dimensional problems ask you to 'look behind what appears on the surface of things'. You have to conceptualize a diagram that exists nowhere else but in your own mind. Generally, people who do well on this test are almost always recognized as intelligent, even if they are unexceptional in their conventional education, so they often do well when they have left school.

TEST 10

FORMATION

This test explores how easily you can 'see' and turn around objects in your mind. You are shown a shape in the middle of the page. Below it are five other shapes. Each of these is numbered. You have to decide whether each of the alternatives is identical to the original shape. It will still be identical to the original if it has been turned over or around. It will not be the same as the original if the proportions or parts have been changed. You are to answer each question with a 'Y' for Yes and 'N' for No. If each shape is not exactly the same or a 'mirror image' you mark 'N' for No. Try to 'see' the shape in your mind.

Example

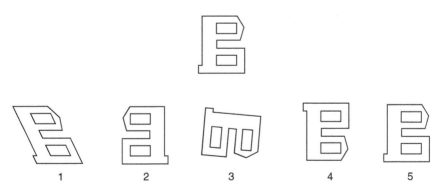

Answers to example items: 1 N;   2 N;   3 Y;   4 Y;   5 Y

Do not mark this book if it is not your own, but record your answers and any working out you need to do on separate paper. If you wish to gain an estimate of your aptitude, record the number of the question you are on after exactly 10 minutes. Otherwise, take as long as you wish to complete the items.

Timed test: 10 minutes

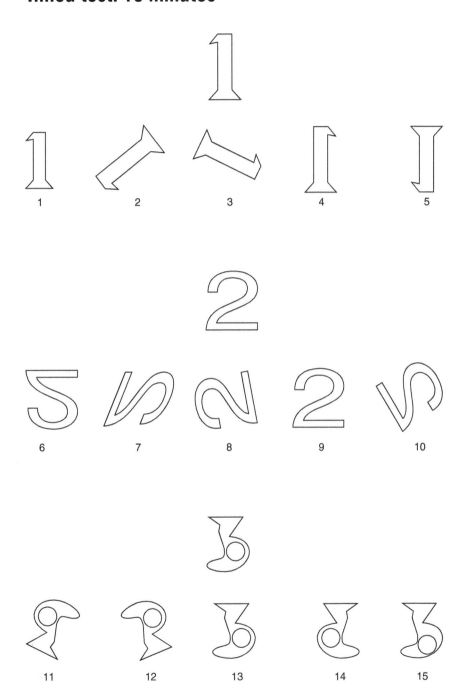

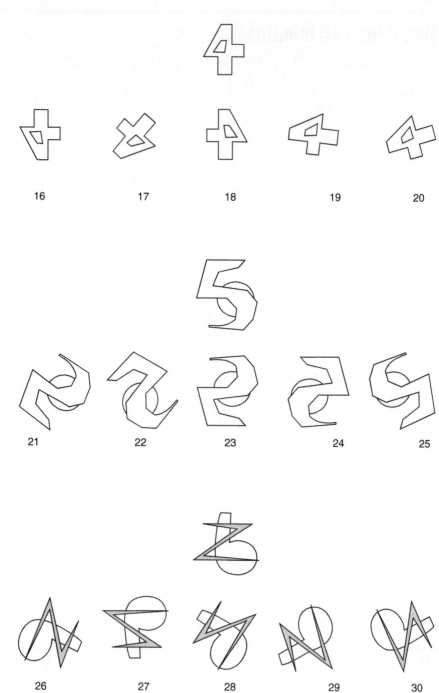

16

17

18

19

20

21

22

23

24

25

26

27

28

29

30

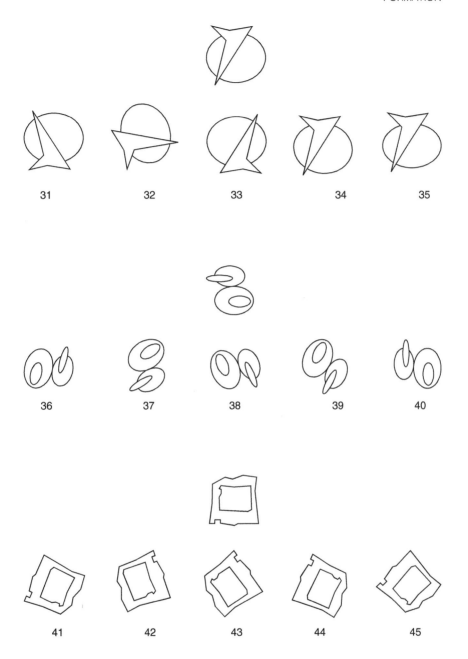

31   32   33   34   35

36   37   38   39   40

41   42   43   44   45

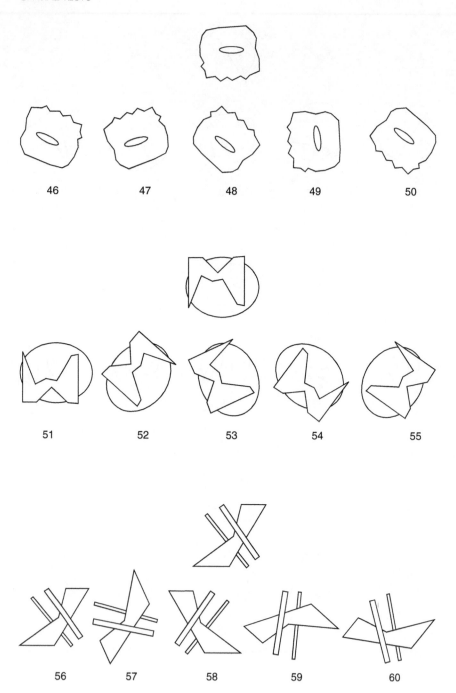

46   47   48   49   50

51   52   53   54   55

56   57   58   59   60

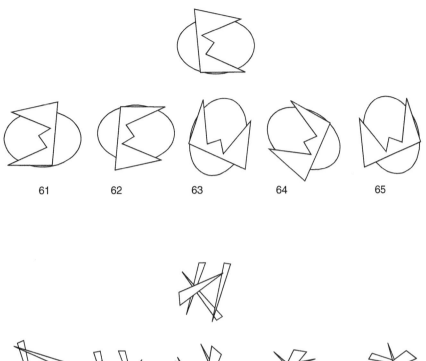

61 62 63 64 65

66 67 68 69 70

Answers

1 N	15 N	29 N	43 Y	57 Y
2 N	16 N	30 Y	44 Y	58 Y
3 Y	17 Y	31 Y	45 N	59 N
4 Y	18 Y	32 N	46 N	60 N
5 Y	19 Y	33 Y	47 Y	61 N
6 Y	20 Y	34 N	48 N	62 N
7 N	21 N	35 N	49 Y	63 Y
8 N	22 Y	36 Y	50 N	64 Y
9 Y	23 N	37 N	51 N	65 Y
10 Y	24 N	38 N	52 N	66 Y
11 Y	25 Y	39 Y	53 N	67 Y
12 N	26 N	40 Y	54 N	68 Y
13 Y	27 Y	41 N	55 Y	69 Y
14 Y	28 Y	42 N	56 Y	70 Y

Scoring

Number right minus number wrong = _____

Plus 2 aged under 16, plus 1 if aged 17–20   + _____

Score on the test = _____

Use the following table to convert your test score to a score out of 10 or 'sten score'. You can then enter your 'sten score' in the chart on page 234.

Test score	1–6	7–12	13–17	18–21	22–25	26–30	31–35	36–41	42–47	48+
Sten score	1	2	3	4	5	6	7	8	9	10

TEST 11

3D TESTS

In this test you are asked to discover the hidden sides of objects. You are shown a stack of blocks. Each block is exactly the same size. You can see the front, or facing, sides. You can also see the top side. But you cannot see the two sides that are hidden from your view. Nor can you see the bottom, or underneath, side. However, you can imagine what the hidden sides and underneath must look like.

In each of the tests, there is a stack of blocks. You have to imagine, out of the five possibilities you are given, which one is the view from Side A. Only one of the five is correct. Then, do the same for Sides B and C. In each set of possibilities, only one is correct, even though it may have been turned around. Tick the correct one.

Timed test: 5 minutes

1

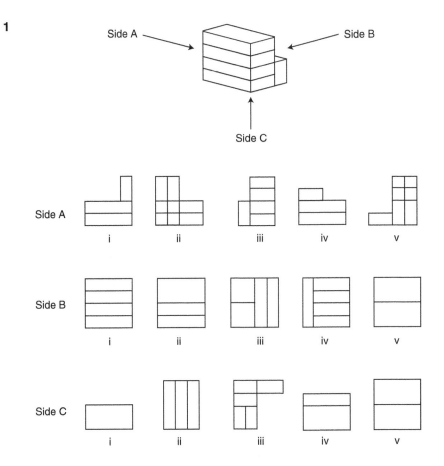

2

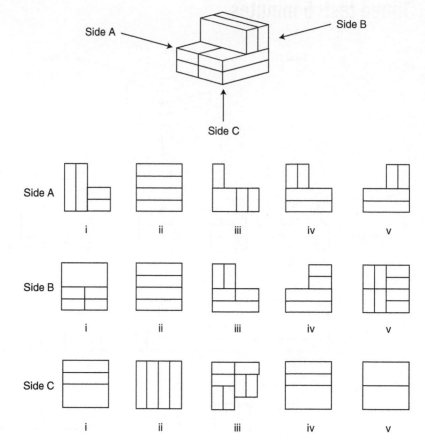

3

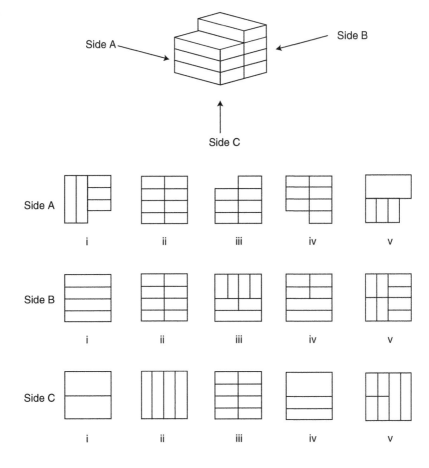

4

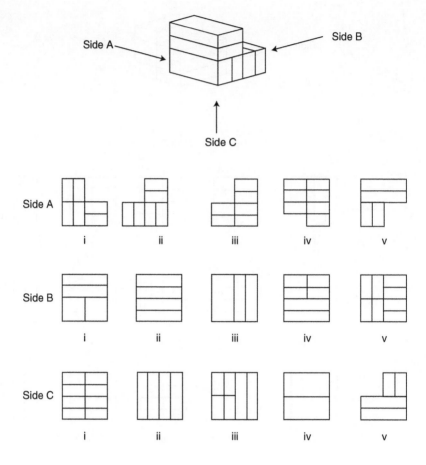

5

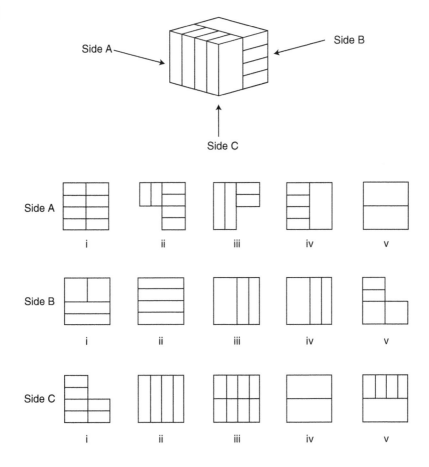

6

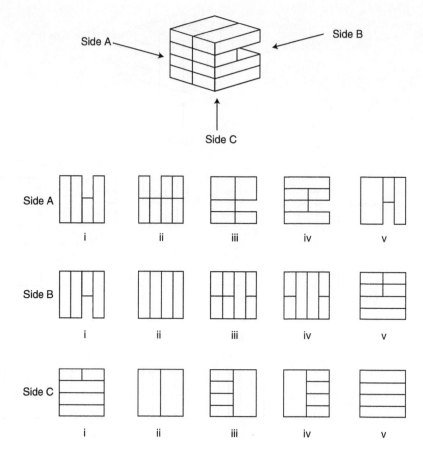

7

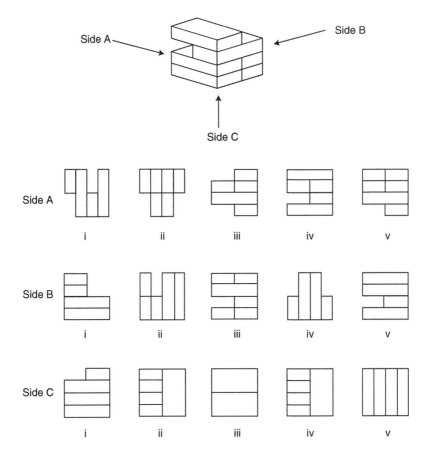

8

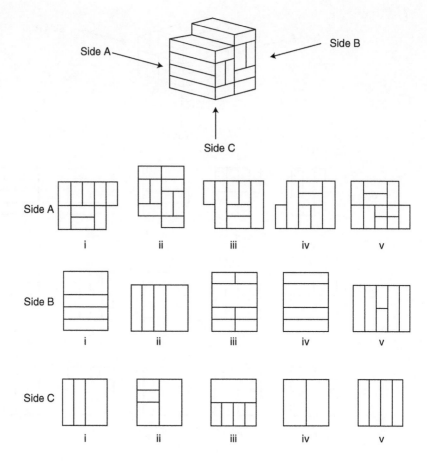

9

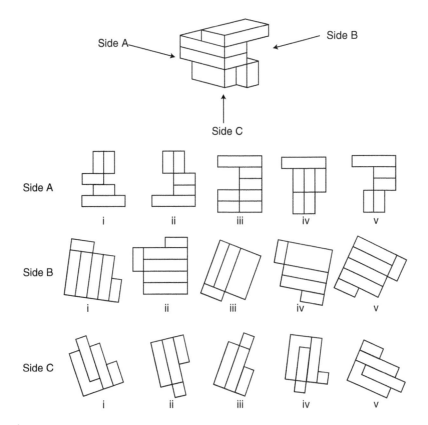

10

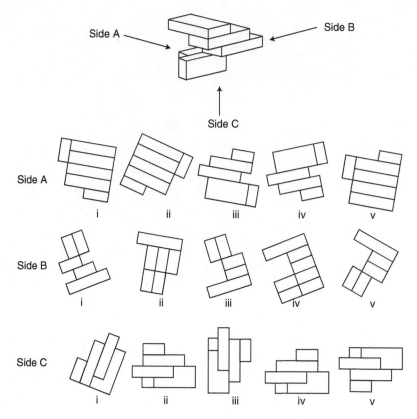

Answers

1	A. iii	B. ii	C. iv
2	A. iv	B. i	C. v
3	A. iv	B. i	C. i
4	A. ii	B. iii	C. ii
5	A. iv	B. ii	C. v
6	A. i	B. iii	C. ii
7	A. v	B. v	C. iii
8	A. ii	B. iv	C. iv
9	A. v	B. iv	C. i
10	A. iii	B. iii	C. v

Scoring

Number right minus number wrong = _____

Plus 3 aged under 16, plus 2 if aged 17–20   + _____

Score on the test = _____

Use the following table to convert your test score to a score out of 10 or 'sten score'. You can then enter your 'sten score' in the chart on page 234.

Test score	1–2	3–4	5–6	7–8	9–10	11–12	13–16	17–19	20–22	23+
Sten score	1	2	3	4	5	6	7	8	9	10

Part Six

Practical numerical tests

This section comprises the largest number of tests, reflecting their importance and the likelihood that these are the ones that most people will encounter. You have to work with the rules of numbers: addition, subtraction, division and multiplication. It is also important to understand decimals, percentages, and fractions.

All of us use figures in relation to our personal finances and in various practical situations where calculating and estimating are a necessary part of daily life. But some people have a liking for this type of activity or a talent for it that then leads them to think of careers in which they are dealing with money, estimating or performing other arithmetical functions. The range of careers that require these skills is vast and also extremely varied.

Many people will declare that these days they leave such figure work to a calculator or to a computer and that therefore they have become 'rusty'. Nevertheless, to do well in this test requires an underlying aptitude, which will appear as an above-average score, even though you may not have used the necessary skills for some time.

Test 12, Reckoning, is designed to assess your numerical agility with the basic rules of numbers. Test 13, Arithmetic, places you in a true-to-life office situation to see how well you can look after money transactions. Test 14, Figure work, is a wide-ranging test that stretches you on fractions and percentages as well as other number problems. Test 15, Number skills, is even more wide ranging as it introduces measurement and asks for answers to practical problems. Test 16, Calculations, asks that you find out what is missing in a series of calculations, which involves checking that answers are correct.

In many careers, the basic calculation has to be 'summed up' quickly, even if it is a rough approximation, so that a decision can be reached in principle. This happens in many areas of financial assessment, costing, and surveying work as well as in buying and selling.

TEST 12

RECKONING

You have to work out sums, using the following rules:

+   means plus, or add;
−   means minus, or take away;
*   means multiplied by, or times;
/   means divided by.

You *must* work out the sums in the order they are written. So, with $3+1*2/2 = ?$:

First step $3+1 = 4$
Second step $4*2 = 8$
Third step $8/2 = 4$

In the examples below, each has three sums. You have to see whether one of the sums gives an answer that is different from the other two, or whether all the answers are the same. Then you have to place a tick in the box by the correct answer. Examples 1 and 2 have been done to show you how. Work out examples 3 and 4 yourself. Mark your answer with a tick.

Example 1	☐ a)	☐ b)	☑ c)	☐ d)
	$1+2 = 3$	$3+0 = 3$	$2+2 = 4$	all the same
Example 2	☐ a)	☐ b)	☐ c)	☑ d)
	$2*2 = 4$	$3+1 = 4$	$6-2 = 4$	all the same
Example 3	☐ a)	☐ b)	☐ c)	☐ d)
	$2/2 =$	$1+1 =$	$6-4 =$	all the same

Example 4   ☐ a)   ☐ b)   ☐ c)   ☐ d)

       $2*2+1 =$ $3+1+1 =$ $4-3*2+3 =$ all the same

Check your answers for examples 3 and 4:

Example 3   ☑ a)   ☐ b)   ☐ c)   ☐ d)

       $2/2 = 1$ $1+1 = 2$ $6-4 = 2$ all the same

Example 4   ☐ a)   ☐ b)   ☐ c)   ☑ d)

       $2*2+1 = 5$ $3+1+1 = 5$ $4-3*2+3 = 5$ all the same

For example 3, you should have placed a tick in the box next to a). For example 4, you should have placed your tick in the box next to d).

Do not mark this book if it is not your own, but record your answers and any working out you need to do on separate paper. If you wish to gain an estimate of your aptitude, record the number of the question you are on after exactly 8 minutes. Otherwise, take as long as you wish to complete the items.

Timed test: 8 minutes

1. ☐ a)
   $2+2 =$
   ☐ b)
   $1+1 =$
   ☐ c)
   $3+1 =$
   ☐ d)
   all the same

2. ☐ a)
   $2+1 =$
   ☐ b)
   $3+1 =$
   ☐ c)
   $2+2 =$
   ☐ d)
   all the same

3. ☐ a)
   $2+2 =$
   ☐ b)
   $3+1 =$
   ☐ c)
   $4+1 =$
   ☐ d)
   all the same

4. ☐ a)
   $2-1 =$
   ☐ b)
   $1+2 =$
   ☐ c)
   $3-2 =$
   ☐ d)
   all the same

5. ☐ a)
   $2+2 =$
   ☐ b)
   $1*4 =$
   ☐ c)
   $4-0 =$
   ☐ d)
   all the same

6. ☐ a)
   $3*2 =$
   ☐ b)
   $5+1 =$
   ☐ c)
   $4*2 =$
   ☐ d)
   all the same

7. ☐ a)
   $2/2 =$
   ☐ b)
   $1+1 =$
   ☐ c)
   $2-1 =$
   ☐ d)
   all the same

8. ☐ a)
   $2*3 =$
   ☐ b)
   $3+1+1 =$
   ☐ c)
   $2+3 =$
   ☐ d)
   all the same

9. ☐ a)
   $2/1 =$
   ☐ b)
   $1+1 =$
   ☐ c)
   $4/2 =$
   ☐ d)
   all the same

10. ☐ a)
    $4*2 =$
    ☐ b)
    $8/2 =$
    ☐ c)
    $4-0 =$
    ☐ d)
    all the same

11. ☐ a)
    $3/1 =$
    ☐ b)
    $1+1+1 =$
    ☐ c)
    $1*3 =$
    ☐ d)
    all the same

12. ☐ a)
    $2*3 =$
    ☐ b)
    $7-1 =$
    ☐ c)
    $6/3 =$
    ☐ d)
    all the same

13. ☐ a)
    $6/2 =$
    ☐ b)
    $9/3 =$
    ☐ c)
    $6-3 =$
    ☐ d)
    all the same

14 ☐ a)   ☐ b)   ☐ c)   ☐ d)
   2*5 =   2*2*2 =   3*2+4 =   all the same

15 ☐ a)   ☐ b)   ☐ c)   ☐ d)
   2/2*3 =   1+1*2 =   6–4*2 =   all the same

16 ☐ a)   ☐ b)   ☐ c)   ☐ d)
   2*3–2 =   3+4–2 =   10/2 =   all the same

17 ☐ a)   ☐ b)   ☐ c)   ☐ d)
   2–2+4 =   1*1+4 =   6–2 =   all the same

18 ☐ a)   ☐ b)   ☐ c)   ☐ d)
   6*2+3 =   3+1*4 =   5*2+5 =   all the same

19 ☐ a)   ☐ b)   ☐ c)   ☐ d)
   9/3*2 =   11+7/3 =   6–1*2 =   all the same

20 ☐ a)   ☐ b)   ☐ c)   ☐ d)
   2*7+2 =   2*2*2 =   1*2*4 =   all the same

21 ☐ a)   ☐ b)   ☐ c)   ☐ d)
   12/3 =   16/4 =   20/5 =   all the same

22 ☐ a)   ☐ b)   ☐ c)   ☐ d)
   20/5–2 =   36/3/6 =   27/3/3 =   all the same

23 ☐ a)   ☐ b)   ☐ c)   ☐ d)
   34/2+3 =   50/5+8 =   60/3–2 =   all the same

24 ☐ a)   ☐ b)   ☐ c)   ☐ d)
   25/5–3 =   6*3/9 =   4*5/10 =   all the same

25 ☐ a)   ☐ b)   ☐ c)   ☐ d)
   6*5/3 =   2*7–2 =   6/2+7 =   all the same

26 ☐ a)   ☐ b)   ☐ c)   ☐ d)
   9*4 =   3*12 =   4*8+6 =   all the same

27 ☐ a)   ☐ b)   ☐ c)   ☐ d)
   17*3–11 =   8*4+8 =   84/2–4 =   all the same

28 ☐ a)   ☐ b)   ☐ c)   ☐ d)
$48/8 =$ $54/9 =$ $49/7 =$ all the same

29 ☐ a)   ☐ b)   ☐ c)   ☐ d)
$101-29/6 =$ $87-53/2 =$ $77-41/3 =$ all the same

30 ☐ a)   ☐ b)   ☐ c)   ☐ d)
$13*3-3 =$ $11*4-6 =$ $16*2+4 =$ all the same

31 ☐ a)   ☐ b)   ☐ c)   ☐ d)
$16/2*3 =$ $8*6/2 =$ $6*4 =$ all the same

32 ☐ a)   ☐ b)   ☐ c)   ☐ d)
$12*3/2 =$ $3*3*2 =$ $40/5*2 =$ all the same

33 ☐ a)   ☐ b)   ☐ c)   ☐ d)
$16*3 =$ $5*5*2 =$ $24/2*4 =$ all the same

34 ☐ a)   ☐ b)   ☐ c)   ☐ d)
$33/3-5 =$ $17+8/5 =$ $19-4/3 =$ all the same

35 ☐ a)   ☐ b)   ☐ c)   ☐ d)
$7*9+7 =$ $6*11+8 =$ $6*9+16 =$ all the same

36 ☐ a)   ☐ b)   ☐ c)   ☐ d)
$84/7/2 =$ $132/11-5 =$ $36*4/24 =$ all the same

37 ☐ a)   ☐ b)   ☐ c)   ☐ d)
$116-77/13 =$ $16*9/48 =$ $93-57/12 =$ all the same

38 ☐ a)   ☐ b)   ☐ c)   ☐ d)
$35/7-2 =$ $17*2-30 =$ $21-9/3 =$ all the same

39 ☐ a)   ☐ b)   ☐ c)   ☐ d)
$29*3-19 =$ $7*14-30 =$ $113-79+34 =$ all the same

40 ☐ a)   ☐ b)   ☐ c)   ☐ d)
$68/17 =$ $90/18 =$ $250/50 =$ all the same

41 ☐ a)   ☐ b)   ☐ c)   ☐ d)
$43*4/43 =$ $88/11/2 =$ $128*3/96 =$ all the same

42 ☐ a)   ☐ b)   ☐ c)   ☐ d)
    $26+51+23/4 =$ $1000/40 =$ $55+13+32/4 =$ all the same

43 ☐ a)   ☐ b)   ☐ c)   ☐ d)
    $898-669 =$ $108+137 =$ $1003-774 =$ all the same

44 ☐ a)   ☐ b)   ☐ c)   ☐ d)
    $1348/337+1 =$ $687/229-1 =$ $1023/341+2 =$ all the same

45 ☐ a)   ☐ b)   ☐ c)   ☐ d)
    $11*21-59/4 =$ $459-63/9 =$ $22*10/5 =$ all the same

Answers

1 b	**11** d	**21** d	**31** d	**41** d
2 a	**12** c	**22** c	**32** c	**42** d
3 c	**13** d	**23** a	**33** b	**43** b
4 b	**14** b	**24** d	**34** a	**44** b
5 d	**15** a	**25** b	**35** b	**45** a
6 c	**16** a	**26** c	**36** b	
7 b	**17** b	**27** c	**37** d	
8 a	**18** b	**28** c	**38** a	
9 d	**19** c	**29** b	**39** d	
10 a	**20** a	**30** b	**40** a	

Scoring

Number right minus number wrong = _____

Plus 2 aged under 16, plus 1 if aged 17–20   + _____

Score on the test = _____

Use the following table to convert your test score to a score out of 10 or 'sten score'. You can then enter your 'sten score' in the chart on page 234.

Test score	1–17	18–20	21–24	25–26	27–28	29–30	31–33	34–35	36–38	39+
Sten score	1	2	3	4	5	6	7	8	9	10

TEST 13

ARITHMETIC

An office keeps a box containing money (a Petty Cash Box) from which small payments can be made. In some offices, this is called a 'float'. When money is taken from the box, a note is left inside the box saying how much has been taken and what it has been taken for. These notes are written either on a Petty Cash Voucher or on a Memo.

You will be asked to do some calculations about the amounts of money that appear on the Vouchers and Memos. You are not allowed calculators or other computing aids. The Vouchers and Memos look like this:

Petty Cash Voucher			☎ MEMO
7 June			I took £10 from petty cash
	£	p	for stamps. I put the change
Expenses for			– £1.00 – back in the box.
Taxi fare	10	00	
Sandwiches	10	00	Jenny
Total	20	00	11 June
Signature: Bob			

Example questions and answers

1   How much did Jenny spend on 11 June?   £9.00

2   What is £1 as a fraction (or part) of £10?   1/10

3   What percentage of Bob's voucher was spent on sandwiches?   50 per cent.

In Question 1, Jenny took £10 and put £1 back, so spent £9. In Question 2, £10 is 10 times as much as £1, so £1 is one tenth of £10. In Question 3, the total was £20 and the sandwiches cost £10, which is 50 per cent of the total.

In the test the Vouchers and Memos give information about how much money has been taken from the box. The money is taken from the box on the date of the Voucher or Memo. At the start of the test you are told how much is in the Petty Cash Box before anybody has taken anything from it.

In the test the answers you get to some of the early items will help you to work out your answers to later ones, so it is best to do the questions in the order they come. Do not mark this book if it is not your own, but record your answers and any working out you need to do on separate paper.

If you wish to gain an estimate of your aptitude, record the number of the question you are on after exactly 15 minutes. Otherwise, take as long as you wish to complete the items.

Timed test: 15 minutes

Petty Cash Voucher		
7 June		
	£	p
Milk	4	25
Sandwiches for JH Group	8	50
Total		
Signature: Christine		

Petty Cash Voucher		
9 June		
	£	p
Expenses for Jane Smith (interviewed 17 June)		
Train (return)	22	60
Midday snack	5	65
Total		
Signature: Sandy		

Petty Cash Voucher		
10 June		
	£	p
Window cleaning:		
week 25th May	22	50
week 1st June	37	50
Total	60	00
Signature: Jack		

Petty Cash Voucher		
10 June		
	£	p
Snacks on 7 June	6	72
Petrol 28 miles at 30p	2	80
Stationery items	18	48
Total	27	00
Signature: John		

Petty Cash Voucher		
11 June		
	£	p
Stationery:		
Photocopying	5	70
Rail Guide	4	10
Stationery	7	00
Milk jug	4	20
Total		
Signature: John		

Petty Cash Voucher		
15 June		
	£	p
Flowers for reception	8	75
Magazines for reception	6	25
Total		
Signature: Christine		

Petty Cash Voucher		
18 June		
	£	p
Petrol expenses:		
29 May 50 miles		
1 June 20 miles		
7 June 34 miles		
16 June 96 miles		
@ 30p per mile		
Total	61	80
Signature: Bill		

Petty Cash Voucher		
22 June		
	£	p
Travel expenses for Mr Curtis (who came for interview on 6 June)	37	00
Total	37	00
Signature: Tom		

Petty Cash Voucher		
22 June		
	£	p
Flowers for lobby	8	70
Sandwiches for JH Group on 5 June	16	10
Taxi to station for PB	8	60
Total	28	40
Signature: Jenny		

Petty Cash Voucher		
23 June		
	£	p
Newspapers	3	30
Magazines for lobby	7	50
Sub total	11	80
Less money not used up on taxi fare on 19 June	1	40
Total	10	40
Signature: Marty		

Petty Cash Voucher 24 June		
	£	p
Flowers for reception	15	60
Flowers for lobby	5	20
Urgent stationery	10	75
Total		
Signature: Jenny		

% MEMO

I have taken £5 from petty cash for a taxi fare.

Marty
19 June

Petty Cash Voucher 24 June		
	£	p
Biscuits	1	86
Sugar	1	54
Tea	2	50
Light bulbs	3	80
Batteries	2	30
Signature: Christine		

% MEMO

I took £5 from petty cash for stamps. I put the change – £1.65 – back in the box.

Jenny
11 June

Take note that a) the Petty Cash Box had £72.30 in it on 1 June; b) payments of £75 each were made into the Petty Cash Box on 6, 13, 20 and 27 June.

1   How many Vouchers and Memos are there in total?_____

2   How many more Vouchers than Memos are there?_____

3   What is the number of Vouchers divided by the number of Memos?_____

4   What was the total of the four payments made into the Petty Cash Box?_____

5   What is £75 as a percentage of the four payments made into Petty Cash?_____

6   What was the total taken by Christine on 7 June?_____

7   What is £4.25 as a percentage of £8.50?_____

8   What was the total taken by Sandy on 9 June?_____

9   What is £5.65 as a percentage of £22.60?_____

10   How much more did Christine spend on flowers than magazines on 15 June?_____

11   How much more did Christine spend on 15 than 24 June?_____

12   What was Christine's total on 24 June as a percentage of her total on 15 June?_____

13   From Jenny's Memo of 11 June, how much did she spend on stamps?_____

14   How much in error was Bill's claim for petrol on 18 June?_____

15   What percentage of Bill's corrected claim for petrol was his expense for 1 June?_____

IMPORTANT: If you have found a voucher or memo that needed to be corrected, use the correct figures for the calculations numbers 16 to 25.

16   What was the accurate total for John's voucher on 10 June?_____

17   What was John's original claim for petrol as a percentage of the correct claim?_____

18   How much less did John spend on 11 June than 10 June?_____

19   What were snacks as a percentage of the total of John's voucher of 10 June?_____

20   What percentage of the window cleaning bill was for May?_____

21   What was Jenny's correct total for 22 June?_____

22   How much did Marty spend from his memo of 19 and voucher of 23 June?_____

23   What percentage of the correct total for 19 and 23 June was the taxi?_____

24   What was the correct amount of expense between 7 and 16 June?_____

25   How much money would have remained in Petty Cash on 1 July?_____

Answers

1 14	**6** £12.75	**11** £3.00	**16** £33.60 (or 33¹/₃)	**21** £33.40
2 10	**7** 50%	**12** 80%	**17** 33.33%	**22** £14.40
3 6 (or ¹/₆)	**8** £28.25	**13** £3.35	**18** £12.60	**23** 25%
4 £300	**9** 25%	**14** £1.80	**19** 20%	**24** £173.95
5 25%	**10** £2.50	**15** 10%	**20** 37.5%	**25** £10

Scoring

Number right minus number wrong = _____

Plus 2 aged under 16, plus 1 if aged 17–20   + _____

Score on the test = _____

Use the following table to convert your test score to a score out of 10 or 'sten score'. You can then enter your 'sten score' in the chart on page 234.

Test score	1–6	7–8	9	10–11	12–13	14–15	16–17	18–19	20–21	22+
Sten score	1	2	3	4	5	6	7	8	9	10

TEST 14

FIGURE WORK

In this test you are asked to work out various sums and calculations. The test involves arithmetic and will also test you on decimals, percentages and fractions. You are not allowed a calculator on this test.

In this test: '+' means add, '–' means take away or subtract, '×' means multiply or times, '/' means divide by.

For each problem write the correct answer in the space provided on the right-hand side. Look at the examples below. The first one has been done for you.

Examples

1   10/2 = ? (Answer: 5)

2   What is 50 per cent of £20? _____

3   What is 3 × ½? _____

4   1.3 – (minus) 0.9 = ? _____

In Example 2, the answer is £10 – 50 per cent is the same as 50 parts out of 100 or the same as five parts in 10. One part in 10 of £20 is £2, so 5 parts is £10.

In Example 3 the answer is 1½. Three half parts make one and a half parts, which is the same as half of three.

In Example 4 the answer is 0.4. This is 13 parts take away 9 parts and then putting back the decimal point in the correct place.

Make sure you have scrap paper for any rough working you may want to do on this test. Please do not mark the book if it is not your own, but record your answers on a separate sheet.

Timed test: 10 minutes

1 $10 - 5 = ?$ _____

2   What is 10% (10 per cent) of £40? _____

3   What is $4 \times$ ½ (half of 4)? _____

4 $1.6 -$ (minus) $0.3 = ?$ _____

5 $21 / 7 = ?$ _____

6   What is 5% of £40? _____

7   What is $8 \times$ ¼? _____

8 $2.1 + 1.9 = ?$ _____

9 $10 \times 13 = ?$ _____

10   What is 3% of £100? _____

11   What is $16 \times$ ¼? _____

12 $3.08 + 2.19 = ?$ _____

13 $156 / 12 = ?$ _____

14   What is $1/3 \times 1/3$? _____

15   What is 7½% of £300? _____

16   What is $15 / 2$½? _____

17 $106.7 - 103.81 = ?$ _____

18   What is 32/50 as a percentage? _____

19   A rectangular floor measures 2.5 metres by 3 metres. What is the size of the floor in square metres? _____

20   What is 22½% of £200? _____

21   What is 4¼ $\times$ ¼? _____

22 0.07×0.02 _____

23 $17 \times 29 = ?$ _____

24   What is 6% of £40 added to 12½% of £20? _____

25   What is 6 divided by 8? _____

26   What is 0.09 divided by 0.3? _____

27 From £50 how much change will you have if you purchase as many items as possible each costing £1.99? _____

28 How many dollars will I get for £10 if the exchange rate is 1.45 dollars to the pound? _____

29 The interest on a £1,000 loan is 20% annually. What is the total amount of interest paid at the end of year two? _____

30 If an item cost £126 when discounted to 60% of its original price what was the original price? _____

Answers

1 5	**7** 2	**13** 13	**19** 7.5	**25** 0.75
2 £4	**8** 4	**14** 1/9	**20** £45	**26** 0.3
3 2	**9** 130	**15** £22.50	**21** 1 and 1/16	**27** 25p
4 1.3	**10** £3	**16** 6	**22** 0.0014	**28** $14.50
5 3	**11** 4	**17** 2.89	**23** 493	**29** £440
6 £2	**12** 5.27	**18** 64%	**24** £4.90	**30** £210

Scoring

Number right minus number wrong = _____

Plus 2 aged under 16, plus 1 if aged 17–20   + _____

Score on the test = _____

Use the following table to convert your test score to a score out of 10 or 'sten score'. You can then enter your 'sten score' in the chart on page 234.

Test score	1–4	5–8	9–12	13–15	16–17	18–19	20–22	23–24	25–26	27+
Sten score	1	2	3	4	5	6	7	8	9	10

Explanations

1
$$10$$
$$- 5$$
$$5$$

2
$$\frac{10}{100} \times \frac{40}{1}$$
$$= \frac{400}{100}$$
$$= £4$$

3 $4 \times \dfrac{1}{2}$
$$= \frac{4}{1} \times \frac{1}{2}$$
$$= \frac{4}{2}$$
$$= 2$$

4
$$1.6$$
$$- 0.3$$
$$1.3$$

5

$7\overline{)21}$ → 3

6

$\dfrac{5}{100} \times \dfrac{40}{1}$

$= \dfrac{200}{100}$

$= £2$

7

$\dfrac{8}{1} \times \dfrac{1}{4}$

$= \dfrac{8}{4}$

$= 2$

8

$\begin{array}{r} 2.1 \\ +\ 1.9 \\ \hline 4.0 \end{array}$

9

$\begin{array}{r} 10 \\ \times\ 13 \\ \hline 100 \\ 30 \\ \hline 130 \end{array}$

10

$\dfrac{3}{100} \times \dfrac{100}{1}$

$= \dfrac{300}{100}$

$= £3$

11

$\dfrac{16}{1} \times \dfrac{1}{4}$

$= \dfrac{16}{4}$

$= 4$

12

$\begin{array}{r} 3.08 \\ +\ 2.19 \\ \hline 5.27 \end{array}$

13

$12\overline{)156}$ → 13

$\begin{array}{r} 12 \\ \hline 36 \end{array}$

14 $\dfrac{1}{3} \times \dfrac{1}{3} = \dfrac{1}{9}$

15 7½% of £100 would be £7.50, so of £300 would be £22.50.

16 $15 \div 2\dfrac{1}{2}$

$= \dfrac{15}{1} \div \dfrac{5}{2}$

$= \dfrac{15}{1} \times \dfrac{2}{5}$

$= \dfrac{30}{5}$

$= 6$

17
$$106.7$$
$$-103.81$$
$$\underline{2.89}$$

18
$$\frac{32}{50} \times \frac{100}{1}$$
$$= \frac{32}{1} \times \frac{2}{1}$$
$$= 64\%$$

19
$$2.5$$
$$\times \quad 3$$
$$\overline{7.5}$$

20 10 % of £200 is £20 and 2½% of £200 is £5, so 22½% is £20 + £20 + £5 = £45

21
$$4\frac{1}{4} \times \frac{1}{4}$$
$$= \frac{17}{4} \times \frac{1}{4}$$
$$= \frac{17}{16}$$
$$= 1\frac{1}{16}$$

22
$$0.07$$
$$\times\, 0.02$$
$$\underline{0.0014}$$

Simply multiply the two figures, 2 and 7, which comes to 14, then fix the decimal point by counting the spaces after the decimal point in the two figures you have multiplied. Two for 0.07 and two for 0.02, totals four. Then count back four figures from the end of the line. Two zeros must be placed in front of the figure 14 to enable correct placing of the decimal point.

23
$$17$$
$$\times\ 29$$
$$340$$
$$153$$
$$\underline{493}$$

17 is multiplied first by 20 and then by nine. To multiply by 20 first place a zero at the right hand side of the line. Then multiply the 17 by 2 so the resulting figure is 17 by 20. Then multiply 17 by 9. Firstly, 7 by 9 is 63 and it is important to place the figure 3 exactly under the last figure, the zero, of the line above in order to make it easy to add the figures later on. Then, 1 by 9 is 9, to which you have to add the 6 from 63, which makes 15. The total is the sum of the lines you have multiplied out separately.

24 6% of £40 is
$$\frac{6}{100}\times\frac{40}{1}$$
$$=\frac{6}{5}\times\frac{2}{1}$$
$$=\frac{12}{5}$$
$$=2\frac{2}{5}$$
$$=£2.40$$

12½% of £20 is
$$\frac{25}{200}\times\frac{20}{1}$$
$$=\frac{25}{10}\times\frac{1}{1}$$
$$=\frac{25}{10}$$
$$=2\frac{5}{10}$$
$$=£2.50$$
Total = £4.90

25 6 divided by 8 is
$$\frac{6}{1}\div\frac{8}{1}$$
$$=\frac{6}{1}\times\frac{1}{8}$$
$$=\frac{3}{1}\times\frac{1}{4}$$
$$=\frac{3}{4}\ \text{ or }\ 0.75$$

$$\begin{array}{r}0.75\\8\overline{)6.00}\\0.\\\overline{60}\\56\\\overline{40}\end{array}$$

26 $.03\overline{)\,.09}$
$$\begin{array}{r}3.00\\3\overline{)9.00}\end{array}$$

To divide a decimal, first make the divisor a whole number. In the case of 0.03 the decimal point is moved two spaces to the right. What is done to one number must also be done to the other, so that two spaces to the right of 0.09 gives a whole number of 9.

27 'Round up' the £1.99 to £2. Dividing this into £50 leaves 25 pence remaining.

28 Multiply the number of dollars to the pound by ten.

29 Year one is

$$\frac{1000}{1} \times \frac{20}{100}$$

$$= \frac{10}{1} \times \frac{20}{1}$$

$$= \frac{200}{1}$$

$$= £200$$

Interest on the principal as well as on the interest is calculated for the second year.

Year two is

$$\frac{1200}{1} \times \frac{20}{100}$$

$$= \frac{12}{1} \times \frac{20}{1}$$

$$= \frac{240}{1}$$

$$= £240$$

The total over two years is £440

30 £126 at 60% was originally

$$\frac{126}{1} \times \frac{100}{60}$$

$$= \frac{126}{1} \times \frac{5}{3}$$

$$= \frac{630}{3}$$

$$= £210$$

TEST 15

NUMBER SKILLS

=	equals, same as, for example, A=B, B=C, therefore A=C
+	addition, plus, for example, £2.50 + £2.50 = £5.00
–	subtraction, taking away, for example, £13.00 – £4.50 = £8.50
× or *	multiplication, times, or by, for example, £5.00 * 3 = £15.00
/	division, dividing, for example, £12.00/4 = £3.00

This is a test of your ability to use numbers in everyday circumstances. You are given a calculation to perform. You then have to choose the correct answer from the alternatives provided for you. You are not allowed a calculator or computer. Underline or tick the correct answer. It is advisable to have a piece of scrap paper and a pencil to do any working out that may be necessary. The examples below have been done already to show you how.

Examples

1 What is £12 (twelve pounds) divided by 2?

a) £3   b) £4   c) £12   d) £6   e) £1

2 What is 1.5 (one point five) and 0.5 (zero point 5)?

a) 4   b) 2.5   c) 5   d) 1   e) 2

3 What is 10% (ten per cent) of 60?

a) 1   b) 6   c) 100   d) 0   e) 40

4 What is ¼ (one quarter) of 8?

a) 1/3   b) 4   c) 5   d) one half   e) 2

The answer to Example 1 is d). There are two lots of £6 in £12. The answer to 2 is e). 1.5 and 0.5 are ways of saying one and a half, and a half. The answer to 3 is b), since 10 per cent is the same as saying 10 parts out of a 100 or 1 part out of 10, and 60 divided by 10 is 6. The answer to 4 is e). A ¼ means 1 part in four; 8 has 2 parts of 4.

If you are timing yourself you have 10 minutes to do as much as you can. Work quickly and accurately. Remember, you are likely to need a piece of scrap paper and a pencil. Begin as soon as you are ready.

Timed test: 10 minutes

1   What is left when 5 is taken away from 17?
a) 12   b) 16   c) 10   d) 13   e) 14

2   What is 1.5 added to 1.5?
a) 1   b) 3   c) 3.5   d) 2   e) 2.5

3   What is 50% of £10?
a) £2   b) £6   c) £1   d) £4   e) £5

4   What is a half plus a quarter?
a) 1½   b) 1¾   c) ¾   d) 2   e) ¼

5   What is 6 divided by 2?
a) 3   b) 2   c) 1/2   d) 1   e) 6

6   What is 1.25 added to 8.75?
a) 9   b) 10   c) 11   d) 9½   e) 11

7   What is 50% of £18.50?
a) £10.50   b) £9.25   c) £8.25   d) £9.50   e) £9

8   What is 1¾ multiplied by 2?
a) 3 and 1/4   b) 3 and 3/4   c) 2 and 1/2
d) 2 and 3/4   e) 3 and 1/2

9   What is 24 divided by 8?
a) 4   b) 3   c) 5   d) 6   e) 2

10 What is 1.3 and 10.3?
a) 10.46   b) 17.6   c) 10.43   d) 11.6   e) 10.8

11 What is 10% of £22.20?
a) £11.10   b) £12.10   c) £2.22   d) £2.10   e) £2.20

12 What is ½ divided by 2?
a) 1/4   b) 8   c) 2   d) 4   e) 1/2

13 What does one person get if £30 is divided among 10 people?
a) £10   b) £2   c) £3   d) £15   e) £5

14   What is 3.6 divided by 3?
   a) 1.4   b) 1.2   c) 10.8   d) 3.2   e) 1.3

15   What is 17½% of £200?
   a) £39   b) £29   c) £70   d) £35   e) £34.50

16   What is ¾ divided by 3?
   a) 1/6   b) 1/12   c) 4   d) 1/4   e) 9

17   16 people each receive £5. What was the total amount before the division?
   a) £70   b) £64   c) £30   d) £60   e) £80

18   What is 7.09 less 2.04?
   a) 5.05   b) 4.03   c) 5.15   d) 4.15   e) 4.05

19   What is 12½% of £96?
   a) £18.20   b) £18   c) £14.40   d) £9.60   e) £12

20   What is a fifth of £65?
   a) £1.30   b) £13   c) £13.50   d) £12.50   e) £11

21   7 people shared the cost of a holiday equally between them. The cost of
   the holiday in total was £1,785. How much did each pay?
   a) £245   b) £235   c) £265   d) £255   e) £112.20

22   What is the total of 8.001, 4.36 and 0.0098?
   a) 13.0709   b) 12.3708   c) 13.2329   d) 12.3709   e) 14.3708

23   A new car costs £18,000. How much does it cost when reduced by 5%?
   a) £17,100   b) £16,200   c) £15,000   d) £17,200   e) £17,400

24   What is 4 and a half plus 3 and five sixths?
   a) 8 and 2/3   b) 7 and 2/3   c) 9 and 2/6
   d) 7 and 1/2   e) 8 and 1/3

25   A person sold a car for £3,550, buying a new car for £16,040. What was
   the difference in price between the two cars?
   a) £12,380   b) £12,590   c) £12,490   d) £11,490   e) £13,490

26   A length of wood measuring 1.2 metres has to be cut into three exactly
   equal pieces each of 285 centimetres. How many centimetres are left over?
   a) 345   b) 245   c) 355   d) 145   e) 385

27 Each article costs £5.70, but a 2% reduction is given on bulk orders of 10 or more. What is the cost of 15?
a) £84.89   b) £84.79   c) £83.79   d) £83.69   e) £73.79

28 What is one seventh of one seventh?
a) 49   b) 1/49   c) 1/7   d) 7   e) 1/14

29 A restaurant bill for two people was £36.30. One person's meal was exactly twice as much as the other's. What was the cost of the cheaper meal?
a) £13.10   b) £26.20   c) £12.15   d) £12.10   e) £12.20

30 The cost of apples is £1.80 per kilo. When the apples weigh 2.8 kilos, what is the total cost?
a) £4   b) £4.84   c) £4.94   d) £5.14   e) £5.04

31 Four children out of a class of 25 were not able to read. What percentage is this?
a) 25%   b) 16%   c) 12%   d) 8%   e) 15%

32 What is 2/5 added to 1/6 and 1/3?
a) 7/8   b) 17/18   c) 29/30   d) 4/5   e) 9/10

33 A group of 8 adults and 16 children paid a total of £5,400 for a holiday. The cost per adult was twice that of each child. What was the cost per child?
a) £540   b) £270   c) £225   d) £168.75   e) £337.50

34 What is 3.073 divided by 0.04?
a) 76.825   b) 7.6825   c) 768.25   d) 7682.5   e) 0.76825

35 What is 27% of £425?
a) £94.75   b) £114.75   c) £104.75   d) £124.75   e) £84.75

36 What is 3/16 of 200 written as a percentage?
a) 62.5%   b) 77.5%   c) 75%   d) 65%   e) 37.5%

37 What is 1,095 multiplied by 13 and divided by 15?
a) 949   b) 1049   c) 948   d) 959   e) 947

38 What is 0.07 divided by 350?
a) 0.2   b) 0.02   c) 0.002   d) 0.0002   e) 2

39 By the time a man decided to buy a house the cost had inflated by around 8% to £182,000. What was the approximate price before inflation?
a) £170,000   b) £167,500   c) £168,500
d) £169,000   e) £159,500

40 What is 3 and 1/2 divided by 2 and 1/4?
a) 6 and 1/8   b) 1 and 1/2   c) 1 and 8/9
d) 1 and 4/5   e) 1 and 5/9

Answers

1 a	6 b	11 c	16 d	21 d	26 a	31 b	36 e
2 b	7 b	12 a	17 e	22 b	27 c	32 e	37 a
3 e	8 e	13 c	18 a	23 a	28 b	33 d	38 d
4 c	9 b	14 b	19 e	24 e	29 d	34 a	39 c
5 a	10 d	15 d	20 b	25 c	30 e	35 b	40 e

Scoring

Number right minus number wrong = _____

Plus 2 aged under 16, plus 1 if aged 17–20 + _____

Score on the test = _____

Use the following table to convert your test score to a score out of 10 or 'sten score'. You can then enter your 'sten score' in the chart on page 234.

Test score	1–2	3–4	5–8	9–12	13–16	17–20	21–25	26–30	31–35	36+
Sten score	1	2	3	4	5	6	7	8	9	10

Explanations

1
$$17 - 5 = 12$$

2
$$1.5 + 1.5 = 3.0$$

3 50% of £10 is the same as ½ of £10
$$\frac{50}{100} \times \frac{10}{1} = \frac{1}{2} \times \frac{10}{1} = \frac{10}{2} = £5$$

4
$$\frac{1}{2} + \frac{1}{4} = \frac{2}{4} + \frac{1}{4} = \frac{3}{4}$$

5
$$2\overline{)6} \; \; ^3$$

6
$$\begin{array}{r} 1.25 \\ +\;\;8.75 \\ \hline 10.00 \end{array}$$

7
$$\frac{50}{100} \times \frac{18.50}{1}$$
$$= \frac{50}{100} \times 18\frac{1}{2}$$
$$= \frac{1}{2} \times \frac{37}{2}$$
$$= \frac{37}{4}$$
$$= 9\frac{1}{4} \text{ or £9.25}$$

8
$$1\frac{3}{4} \times \frac{2}{1}$$
$$= \frac{7}{4} \times \frac{2}{1}$$
$$= \frac{14}{4}$$
$$= \frac{7}{2}$$
$$= 3\frac{1}{2}$$

9
$$8\overline{)24} \; \; ^3$$

10
$$\begin{array}{r} 1.3 \\ +\;10.3 \\ \hline 11.6 \end{array}$$

11 10% of £22.20 is one-tenth of the total and, as the total is a decimal, the decimal point can be moved one figure to the left, which gives £2.22.

12 ½ divided by 2 is
$$\frac{1}{2} \div \frac{2}{1}$$
$$= \frac{1}{2} \times \frac{1}{2}$$
$$= \frac{1}{4}$$

13 One tenth of £30 is
$$\frac{1}{10} \times \frac{30}{1}$$
$$= \frac{30}{10}$$
$$= \frac{3}{1}$$
$$= 3$$

14
$$3\overline{)3.6} \; \; ^{1.2}$$

15   17½% of £200 is

$$\frac{35}{200} \times \frac{200}{1}$$

$$= \frac{35}{1} \times \frac{1}{1}$$

$$= \frac{35}{1}$$

$$= £35$$

16   ¾ divided by 3 is

$$\frac{3}{4} \div \frac{3}{1}$$

$$= \frac{3}{4} \times \frac{1}{3}$$

$$= \frac{1}{4} \times \frac{1}{1}$$

$$= \frac{1}{4}$$

17
$$\begin{array}{r} 16 \\ \times\ 5 \\ \hline 80 \end{array}$$

18
$$\begin{array}{r} 7.09 \\ -\ 2.04 \\ \hline 5.05 \end{array}$$

19   12½% of £96 is

$$\frac{25}{200} \times \frac{96}{1}$$

$$= \frac{1}{8} \times \frac{96}{1}$$

$$= \frac{1}{1} \times \frac{12}{1}$$

$$= £12$$

20   A fifth (⅕) of £65 is

$$\frac{1}{5} \times \frac{65}{1}$$

$$= \frac{1}{1} \times \frac{13}{1}$$

$$= £13$$

21
$$\begin{array}{r} 255 \\ 7\overline{)1785} \\ 14 \\ \hline 38 \\ 35 \\ \hline 35 \end{array}$$

22
$$\begin{array}{r} 8.001 \\ +\ 4.36 \\ +\ 0.0098 \\ \hline 12.3708 \end{array}$$

23 95% of £18000 is

$$\frac{95}{100} \times \frac{18000}{1}$$

$$= \frac{95}{1} \times \frac{180}{1}$$

$$= £17100 \text{ or by}$$

$$
\begin{array}{r}
180 \\
\times \quad 95 \\
\hline
16200 \\
900 \\
\hline
17100 \\
\end{array}
$$

24 4½ plus 3⅚ is

$$4\frac{1}{2} + 3\frac{5}{6}$$

$$= 7\frac{1}{2} + \frac{5}{6}$$

$$= 7\frac{3}{6} + \frac{5}{6}$$

$$= 7\frac{8}{6}$$

$$= 8\frac{2}{6}$$

$$= 8\frac{1}{3}$$

(When adding fractions, add the whole numbers first.)

25
$$
\begin{array}{r}
16040 \\
- \quad 3550 \\
\hline
12490 \\
\end{array}
$$

26 285 centimetres by 3 = 855 and 1200 less 855 = 345 centimetres.

27
$$
\begin{array}{r}
5.70 \\
\times \quad 15 \\
\hline
5700 \\
2850 \\
\hline
85.50 \\
\end{array}
$$

98% of £85.50 is

$$\frac{98}{100} \times 85\frac{1}{2}$$

$$= \frac{98}{100} \times \frac{171}{2}$$

$$= \frac{49}{100} \times \frac{171}{1}$$

28 $\dfrac{1}{7} \times \dfrac{1}{7} = \dfrac{1}{49}$

29 One person caused two out of the three parts of the bill. Dividing the bill by three gives one part of the bill.

30

$$
\begin{array}{r}
2.8 \\
\times\ 1.8 \\
\hline
280 \\
224 \\
\hline
5.04
\end{array}
$$

31

$$\frac{4}{1} \times \frac{100}{25}$$

$$= \frac{4}{1} \times \frac{4}{1}$$

$$= \frac{16}{1}$$

$$= 16$$

32

$$\frac{2}{5} + \frac{1}{6} + \frac{1}{3}$$

$$= \frac{12}{30} + \frac{5}{30} + \frac{10}{30}$$

$$= \frac{27}{30}$$

$$= \frac{9}{10}$$

(Adding fractions requires a 'common denominator'.)

33 The cost of 8 adults would be the same as for 16 children, so that the total can be regarded as the equivalent of 32 children. £5400 divided by 32 is

$$\frac{5400}{32}$$

or $\dfrac{2700}{16}$

or $\dfrac{1350}{8}$

or $\dfrac{675}{4}$

$= £168.75$

34 $0.04\overline{)3.073}$ is made simpler by

$4\overline{)307.3}$

thus $4\overline{)307.000}$ ... 076.825

$$
\begin{array}{ll}
\underline{28} & \text{(by 7)} \\
27 & \\
\underline{24} & \text{(by 6)} \\
33 & \\
\underline{32} & \text{(by 8)} \\
10 & \\
\underline{8} & \text{(by 2)} \\
20 & \\
20 & \text{(by 5)}
\end{array}
$$

35 27% of £425

is $\dfrac{27}{100} \times \dfrac{425}{1}$

$= \dfrac{27}{4} \times \dfrac{17}{1}$

$= \dfrac{459}{4}$

$= £114.75$

36 $\dfrac{3}{16} \times \dfrac{200}{1}$

$= \dfrac{3}{4} \times \dfrac{50}{1}$

$= \dfrac{150}{4}$

$= 37\dfrac{2}{4}$

$= 37\frac{1}{2}\%$ or 37.5%

37
$$
\begin{array}{r}
1095 \\
\times\quad 13 \\
\hline
10950 \\
3285 \\
\hline
14235
\end{array}
$$

$$
\begin{array}{r}
949 \\
\hline
15)\overline{14235}
\end{array}
$$

38 $\overset{0.0002}{350)\overline{0.0700}}$ Two zeros are added after the 7 to enable 350 to divide into 0.07.

39 $\dfrac{182000}{1} \times \dfrac{100}{108}$

$= 168518.52$

$= $ approx. £168500

40 $3\dfrac{1}{2} \div 2\dfrac{1}{4}$

$= \dfrac{7}{2} \div \dfrac{9}{4}$

$= \dfrac{7}{2} \times \dfrac{4}{9}$

$= \dfrac{28}{18}$

$= 1\dfrac{10}{18}$

$= 1\dfrac{5}{9}$

TEST 16

CALCULATIONS

In this test you are given a sum from which you have to work out the figure that is missing. You have to choose the correct answer from the five alternatives provided. (Remember that + means add, – means take away, * means multiply and / means divide.)

You can mark your answer on the page in the way that suits you best. You can cross the correct answer through, mark with a tick, circle or underline. It is best to mark your answer with a pencil so that you can erase it if you change your mind. Have some spare paper available in case you need it for any rough work.

Examples – what is the missing figure?

1 9/3 = ?

3	4	9	527
a	b	c	d

2 12 * ? = 24

7	24	2	86
a	b	c	d

3 £5.00/2 = ?

£0.5	£1	£2.50	£1.50	£10
a	b	c	d	e

4 £1.50 + £2.00 + ? = £6.00

£2	£1.50	£1	£2.50	£0.50
a	b	c	d	e

In the first example the number 9 divided by 3 gives 3. In the second example 12 is multiplied by 2 to give 24. In the third example £5.00 divided by 2 gives £2.50. In the fourth example £2.50 has to be added to £1.50 and £2.00 to make £6.00.

This test lasts 12 minutes. You have to work accurately and do as many questions as you can in the time allowed. When you are ready, turn over the page and start your timer as you do so.

Timed test: 12 minutes

What is the missing figure?

1   6 + 9 = ?

14	15	3	17	18
a	b	c	d	e

2   11 + ? = 23

12	14	6	10	11
a	b	c	d	e

3   ? – 4 = 3

8	1	7	9	6
a	b	c	d	e

4   12/2 = ?

1	8	4	24	6
a	b	c	d	e

5   ?/8 = 2

16	4	12	2	8
a	b	c	d	e

6   5 * ? = 35

3	9	6	7	5
a	b	c	d	e

7   15 + ? + 15 = 40

24	5	20	10	15
a	b	c	d	e

8   16 * ? = 48

2	32	8	4	3
a	b	c	d	e

9   35 – ? = 19

16	21	26	54	70
a	b	c	d	e

10 ?/7 = 13

81	19	13	91	61
a	b	c	d	e

11 38* 7 = ?

196	166	266	264	164
a	b	c	d	e

12 ? – 94 = 167

198	261	241	291	271
a	b	c	d	e

13 £6.50 + ? = £10

£2.50	£4.50	£1.50	£2.00	£3.50
a	b	c	d	e

14 £9.75 – ? = £5.95

£1.80	£3.80	£1.90	£3.20	£4.20
a	b	c	d	e

15 ? * 9 = 216

24	23	14	34	22
a	b	c	d	e

16 217 + 318 + ? = 1006

371	605	535	471	392
a	b	c	d	e

17 39 * ? = 351

12	8	9	10	11
a	b	c	d	e

18 1091 – ? = 892

199	99	209	189	210
a	b	c	d	e

19 7.5/3 = ?

22.5	21.5	2.5	3.5	2.00
a	b	c	d	e

20   4.9 * ? = 29.4

6.1	5.5	2.5	7	6
a	b	c	d	e

21   51.2 + 38.9 + ? = 101.5

22.8	11.4	10.6	11.2	12.4
a	b	c	d	e

22   £13.91 – ? = £9.64

£4.23	£4.33	£5.27	£3.27	£4.27
a	b	c	d	e

23   ? * 10.5 = 210

20.5	40	30	20	15
a	b	c	d	e

24   ?/4 = £11.05

£44.20	£28.20	£40.20	£45	£46
a	b	c	d	e

25   £20 * 10% = ?

£1	£10	£0.20	£2	£2.20
a	b	c	d	e

26   £24.5 + ? + £107.77 = £299.81

£167.54	£268.67	£168.64	£167.20	£158.94
a	b	c	d	e

27   ? * 25% = £37.50

£115	£150	£75	£18.75	£75.25
a	b	c	d	e

28   ? * 7.3 = 424.13

57.1	57.9	58.1	59.1	56.1
a	b	c	d	e

29   £76 * 15 = ?

£980	£1040	£1220	£1340	£1140
a	b	c	d	e

30 ?/11 = £114.60

£1060.40   £1160.40   £1260.60   £1140.60   £1160.60
a   b   c   d   e

31 £151.91 + £263.87 + £23.99 = ?

£429.77   £439.77   £469.67   £429.77   £439.87
a   b   c   d   e

Answers

1 b	6 d	11 c	16 d	21 b	26 a	31 b
2 a	7 d	12 b	17 c	22 e	27 b	
3 c	8 e	13 e	18 a	23 d	28 c	
4 e	9 a	14 b	19 c	24 a	29 e	
5 a	10 d	15 a	20 e	25 d	30 c	

Scoring

Number right minus number wrong = _____

Plus 2 aged under 16, plus 1 if aged 17–20   + _____

Score on the test = _____

Use the following table to convert your test score to a score out of 10 or 'sten score'. You can then enter your 'sten score' in the chart on page 234.

Test score	1–3	4	5–6	7–8	9–10	11–12	13–14	15–17	18–21	22+
Sten score	1	2	3	4	5	6	7	8	9	10

Part Seven
System tests

Both tests in this section are demanding of your aptitude for quick decision making whilst maintaining absolute concentration. Accuracy is essential. The process mirrors what happens in many forms of programming and operations work where once an error slips in, it becomes difficult, time-consuming and costly to go back and 'unearth' the problem. Thus, the approach you take to these tests can be revealing. For example, even though you may get a high score because of your natural intelligence, psychologists will look carefully at whether you also made a lot of errors, as this may count against you for some tasks where accuracy, though slow, is preferable to quantity that is unreliable.

Test 17, Systems, assesses your effectiveness in converting one set of data into another. Most people check off one symbol at a time as they appear and this is a good way to establish accuracy and organization because the occasional error, even if it does appear, is not likely to appear again. This is not always the case when a person memorizes the symbol and its letter; whilst quicker, any error can get built into the process so that a whole sequence of errors can arise. An advantage of the memorization approach is that it can help with 'problem resolution' where errors may be discovered by scanning the process rather than checking each item individually.

The same remarks are relevant to Test 18, Coding, although this test is different in that the answer is always new and will always make recognizable sense. However, even if the answer may be guessed part-way through the problem-solving process, it still has to be confirmed.

The aptitudes measured in this section are desirable in careers involving financial transactions, legal work and many areas of administration. This type of aptitude, especially as revealed by Test 18, is also demanded in computer programming, analysis and web design.

TEST 17

SYSTEMS

In this test you are given a series of letters and symbols in a row. Each letter goes with a particular symbol. The letter is in the top box of each pair and the symbol is at the bottom.

Your task is to write in the letter that goes with each symbol. The example below shows you how. The first nine boxes in the example have been done already. Complete the last three yourself.

Example

A	B	C	D	E	F	G	H	I	J	K	L
✈	☦	☞	🕯	❄	✡	✝	✋	⚑	💣	☯	☪

Example answer

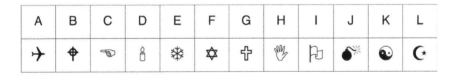

The answers to 10, 11 and 12 are C, A and B.

For each row of letters and symbols, look at each symbol and the letter above it. Then write in the missing letter that goes with each symbol for each of the test items. It is important to do this as quickly as possible without making mistakes.

Do not mark this book if it is not your own, but record your answers and any working out you need to do on separate paper. If you wish to gain an estimate of your aptitude, record the number of the question you are on after exactly 4 minutes. Otherwise, take as long as you wish to complete the items.

Timed test: 4 minutes

A	B	C	D	E	F	G	H	I	J	K	L
✈	☦	☞	🕯	❄	✡	✝	✋	⚑	💣	☯	☪

1	2	3	4	5	6	7	8	9	10	11	12
☪	✈	💣	✋	⚑	❄	✈	✋	☪	☦	✈	🕯

13	14	15	16	17	18	19	20	21	22	23	24
⚑	✋	🕯	☪	⚑	✡	☪	☞	⚑	☦	❄	✡

25	26	27	28	29	30	31	32	33	34	35	36
☪	☯	☞	✡	☪	✈	⚑	❄	✝	✋	💣	✈

37	38	39	40	41	42	43	44	45	46	47	48
✡	💣	✝	☪	🕯	☦	☯	💣	❄	✡	🕯	☞

49	50	51	52	53	54	55	56	57	58	59	60
☯	❄	⚑	🕯	☯	✡	✈	☞	✝	☪	💣	✝

A	B	C	D	E	F	G	H	I	J	K	L
✈	☥	☞	🕯	❄	✡	✝	✋	⚑	💣	☯	☪

61	62	63	64	65	66	67	68	69	70	71	72
✝	✡	✋	☯	☯	☥	💣	🕯	☪	✝	✈	☞

73	74	75	76	77	78	79	80	81	82	83	84
🕯	✋	✝	⚑	☥	☪	☯	❄	☪	⚑	✡	🕯

85	86	87	88	89	90	91	92	93	94	95	96
✡	💣	✈	✋	☪	☯	❄	✈	☥	✋	🕯	✝

97	98	99	100	101	102	103	104	105	106	107	108
✋	✡	⚑	☥	☪	🕯	⚑	☪	✈	☥	💣	✋

109	110	111	112	113	114	115	116	117	118	119	120
☯	💣	☥	✈	✝	⚑	❄	💣	✋	✡	🕯	✝

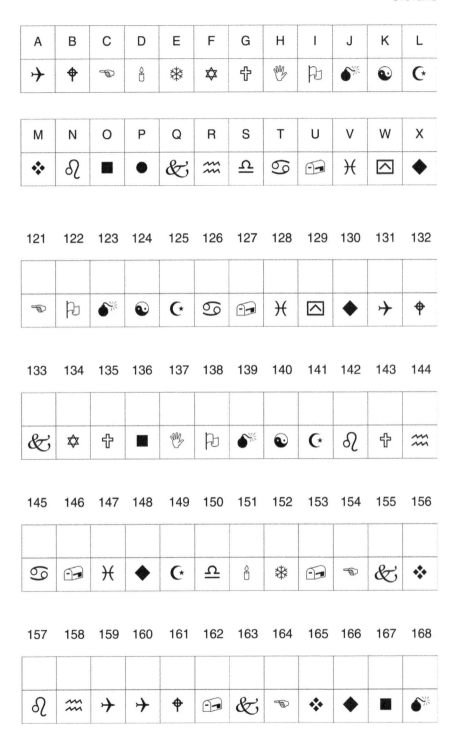

A	B	C	D	E	F	G	H	I	J	K	L
✈	☧	☞	🕯	❄	✡	✝	✋	⚑	💣	☯	☪

M	N	O	P	Q	R	S	T	U	V	W	X
❖	♌	■	●	&	♒	♎	♋	📫	♓	⌂	◆

169	170	171	172	173	174	175	176	177	178	179	180
&	☪	♒	📫	♌	&	■	⚑	💣	✡	✋	♎

181	182	183	184	185	186	187	188	189	190	191	192
◆	✡	✝	✋	■	✈	☪	🕯	❄	&	❖	☞

193	194	195	196	197	198	199	200	201	202	203	204
📫	♌	♎	☞	❖	☪	◆	♒	✋	⚑	💣	■

205	206	207	208	209	210	211	212	213	214	215	216
◆	❖	☞	📫	♎	✈	☞	🕯	☪	🕯	❄	♒

Answers

It is rare for people who have approached this test seriously to have made more than an occasional error, so the number of items you have attempted will provide an overall reliable score. If you think you have been guessing you should check your answers and, after allowing yourself two errors, take away any more errors from the number attempted.

Scoring

Number right minus number wrong = _____ (if more than 3 errors)

Use the following table to convert your test score to a score out of 10 or 'sten score'. You can then enter your 'sten score' in the chart on page 234.

Test score	1–10	11–25	26–40	41–55	56–70	71–90	91–110	111–130	131–149	150+
Sten score	1	2	3	4	5	6	7	8	9	10

TEST 18

CODING

This is a test of how quickly you can form the correct word from drawings or symbols. You are given a line of symbols from which you have to work out the correct word, making use of a chart. You have to write in the correct word in the space provided.

It is best to mark your answer with a pencil so that you can erase it if you change your mind. Examples 1 and 2 below have been done already.

Chart

4	5	6	0	=	Θ	E	P	O	[	Σ	Γ	ϑ
A	B	C	D	E	F	G	H	I	J	K	L	M
Λ	ε	∴	Ξ	ζ	N	1	φ	−	λ	α	γ	M
N	O	P	Q	R	S	T	U	V	W	X	Y	Z

Examples

1   Θ46 =   <u>F A C E</u>

2   γεφ   <u>Y O U</u>

3   NO1   _____

4   4Oζ   _____

In the third example the answer is SIT and in the fourth example the answer is AIR.

This test lasts 6 minutes. You have to work accurately and do as many as you can in the time allowed. Do not mark this book if it is not your own, but record your answers and any working out you need to do on separate paper. If you wish to gain an estimate of your aptitude, record the number of the question you are on after exactly 6 minutes. Otherwise, take as long as you wish to complete the items.

Timed test: 6 minutes

Chart

4	5	6	0	=	Θ	E	P	O	[	Σ	Γ	ϑ
A	B	C	D	E	F	G	H	I	J	K	L	M

Λ	ε	∴	Ξ	ζ	N	1	φ	−	ι	α	γ	M
N	O	P	Q	R	S	T	U	V	W	X	Y	Z

1 400 _____

2 Eε _____

3 5ει _____

4 6ζγ _____

5 0O∴ _____

6 ΘO5 _____

7 E4∴ _____

8 ϑOα _____

9 ∴4γ _____

10 MO∴ _____

4	5	6	0	=	Θ	E	P	O	[	Σ	Γ	ϑ
A	B	C	D	E	F	G	H	I	J	K	L	M
Λ	ε	∴	Ξ	ζ	N	1	φ	–	ι	α	γ	M
N	O	P	Q	R	S	T	U	V	W	X	Y	Z

11   ιOΓ0   _____

12   φEΓγ   _____

13   14ΓΣ   _____

14   ζ4-=   _____

15   ∴ζε0   _____

16   ΞφO∴   _____

17   O0εΓ   _____

18   E4ιΣ   _____

19   0=Λ1   _____

20   Eζ=γ   _____

4	5	6	0	=	Θ	E	P	O	[	Σ	Γ	ϑ
A	B	C	D	E	F	G	H	I	J	K	L	M
Λ	ε	∴	Ξ	ζ	N	1	φ	−	ι	α	γ	M
N	O	P	Q	R	S	T	U	V	W	X	Y	Z

21   =αOΓ=   _____

22   ∴ζOM=   _____

23   ΘΓφNP   _____

24   ϑεζ14Γ   _____

25   Pφϑ5Γγ   _____

26   0ON64ζ0   _____

27   0=ΛOM=Λ   _____

28   OΛNφζ=   _____

29   ΘφN6εφN   _____

30   N4Γϑ4EφΛ0O   _____

Answers

1 ADD	11 WILD	21 EXILE
2 GO	12 UGLY	22 PRIZE
3 BOW	13 TALK	23 FLUSH
4 CRY	14 RAVE	24 MORTAL
5 DIP	15 PROD	25 HUMBLY
6 FIB	16 QUIP	26 DISCARD
7 GAP	17 IDOL	27 DENIZEN
8 MIX	18 GAWK	28 INSURE
9 PAY	19 DENT	29 FUSCOUS
10 ZIP	20 GREY	30 SALMAGUNDI

Scoring

Number right minus number wrong = _____

Plus 2 aged under 16, plus 1 if aged 17–20   + _____

Score on the test =   _____

Use the following table to convert your test score to a score out of 10 or 'sten score'. You can then enter your 'sten score' in the chart on page 234.

Test score	1–3	4–5	6–7	8–9	10–12	13–15	16–17	18–19	20–21	22+
Sten score	1	2	3	4	5	6	7	8	9	10

Part Eight
Practical
verbal tests

All three tests in this section seek to assess your ability to use the English language effectively. Basic skills are, quite rightly, necessary for many jobs, so spelling is an essential. This is not always a requirement, however, where comprehension may be the important thing. In this case, the tests are measuring more abstract potential for reasoning with the meanings of words. This is a requirement in many careers, especially high-level, professional and managerial ones, where understanding the implications of what is being said or written, together with any innuendo, is essential. Language tests are often the most complex, because a word may be used in many different ways. Words are 'slippery', having alternative, deeper or hidden meanings.

Test 19, Word usage, is a test of comprehension and spelling, and how well you understand words. Test 20, Vocabulary, deliberately stretches your vocabulary. It is the type of test that may be given to 'high flyers' who are applying for executive administrative positions. In Test 21, Verbal precision, vocabulary is again important as an excellent indication of your potential for reasoning with words. Clearly, your level and type of education are important here, so that English graduates, who have studied the language and its literature intensely, would be expected to achieve above-average results.

If you do well in these tests there are many careers available to you, particularly in areas where written communication is important, such as journalism, public relations, advertising and administrative roles.

TEST 19

WORD USAGE

In this test you are asked to choose the correct word from those given. You have to tick the box under the correct word. Look at the examples below. Examples 1 and 2 have been done to show you how. Answer the other examples for yourself by placing a tick in the correct box.

Example 1

A piano is a large, musical _____ . Which word should go in the missing space?

country	instrument	ship	band	animal
☐ a)	☐ b)	☐ c)	☐ d)	☐ e)

Example 2

Which word has the incorrect spelling?

national	comment	bargain	certan	friend
☐ a)	☐ b)	☐ c)	☐ d)	☐ e)

Example 3

Which word is the odd one out?

argue	clash	agree	fight	dispute
☐ a)	☐ b)	☐ c)	☐ d)	☐ e)

Example 4

What is the second word in this jumbled sentence when it is in the proper order?

machine	a	is	helicopter	flying
☐ a)	☐ b)	☐ c)	☐ d)	☐ e)

In Example 1, a piano is a large musical 'instrument'. In Example 2, the correct spelling is 'certain' so d is incorrect. In Example 3, the odd one out is 'agree'. All the other words are about disagreement. In Example 4, the correct order for the sentence is: 'A helicopter is a flying machine.' The second word is 'helicopter'. (Although it is possible to have other sentences, 'A flying machine is a helicopter' or 'A machine is a flying helicopter', neither of these is as sensible as: 'A helicopter is a flying machine.')

Do not mark this book if it is not your own, but record your answers and any working out you need to do on separate paper. If you wish to gain an estimate of your aptitude, record the number of the question you are on after exactly 8 minutes. Otherwise, take as long as you wish to complete the items.

Timed test: 8 minutes

1   Cycling is a _____. Which word goes in the missing space?

wheel	sport	window	machine	fish
☐ a)	☐ b)	☐ c)	☐ d)	☐ e)

2   Which word has the incorrect spelling?

traveling	offering	fastened	forbidden	apply
☐ a)	☐ b)	☐ c)	☐ d)	☐ e)

3   Which word is the odd one out?

correct	genuine	real	untrue	honest
☐ a)	☐ b)	☐ c)	☐ d)	☐ e)

4   If the first word is 'Biology' what is the second word?

life the science of is biology.

the	science	is	of	life
☐ a)	☐ b)	☐ c)	☐ d)	☐ e)

5   First aid is help given to an ___ person.

unhelpful	intoxicated	unqualified	injured	impoverished
☐ a)	☐ b)	☐ c)	☐ d)	☐ e)

6   Which word has the incorrect spelling?

lonely	rebellious	February	misprint	adress
☐ a)	☐ b)	☐ c)	☐ d)	☐ e)

7   Which word is the odd one out?

drop	hasten	surge	spring	rush
☐ a)	☐ b)	☐ c)	☐ d)	☐ e)

8   What is the first word in this jumbled sentence when it is in the proper order?

Cuba for is famous tobacco.

famous	Cuba	is	tobacco	for
☐ a)	☐ b)	☐ c)	☐ d)	☐ e)

9   Pipelines can ___ water or oil over great distances.

roll	pull	lift	push	carry
☐ a)	☐ b)	☐ c)	☐ d)	☐ e)

10   Which word has the incorrect spelling?

drinkible	legible	permissible	contemptible	sociable
☐ a)	☐ b)	☐ c)	☐ d)	☐ e)

11   Which word is the odd one out?

indifferent	casual	mindful	careless	neglectful
☐ a)	☐ b)	☐ c)	☐ d)	☐ e)

12   What is the first word in this jumbled sentence when it is in the proper order?
of Italy consists a and islands peninsula.

consists	islands	peninsula	of	Italy
☐ a)	☐ b)	☐ c)	☐ d)	☐ e)

13   A formula is a set form of words or symbols in which something is ___.

used	defined	recommended	corrected	concealed
☐ a)	☐ b)	☐ c)	☐ d)	☐ e)

14   Which word has the incorrect spelling?

paralysis	negociate	embarrass	questionable	immediately
☐ a)	☐ b)	☐ c)	☐ d)	☐ e)

15   Which word is the odd one out?

incompatible	contrasted	unequal	similar	diverse
☐ a)	☐ b)	☐ c)	☐ d)	☐ e)

16   If the last word is 'sun,' what is the third word when these words make a proper sentence?
a sun revolves planet the round.

revolves	a	round	planet	the
☐ a)	☐ b)	☐ c)	☐ d)	☐ e)

17 Breathing ___ allows people to work in a poisoned atmosphere.

involuntarily	mechanically	apparatus	harness	intermittently
☐ a)	☐ b)	☐ c)	☐ d)	☐ e)

18 Which word has the incorrect spelling?

breathe	secretery	delinquent	tolerant	receipt
☐ a)	☐ b)	☐ c)	☐ d)	☐ e)

19 Which word is the odd one out?

burnish	lustre	tarnish	polish	shine
☐ a)	☐ b)	☐ c)	☐ d)	☐ e)

20 What is the second word in this jumbled sentence when it is in the proper order?

business an sound efficient is financially.

financially	efficient	is	an	sound
☐ a)	☐ b)	☐ c)	☐ d)	☐ e)

21 Bacteria can ___ food and spread disease.

analyse	cover	sanitise	eliminate	contaminate
☐ a)	☐ b)	☐ c)	☐ d)	☐ e)

22 Which word has the incorrect spelling?

observant	implement	repellent	environment	committment
☐ a)	☐ b)	☐ c)	☐ d)	☐ e)

23 Which word is the odd one out?

rebellious	amenable	tame	cultivated	ordered
☐ a)	☐ b)	☐ c)	☐ d)	☐ e)

24 If the first word is 'Plastics,' what is the sixth word when the following words make a sentence?

Plastics heat and pressure are materials moulded by that are.

heat	are	moulded	pressure	materials
☐ a)	☐ b)	☐ c)	☐ d)	☐ e)

25 In engineering, a ___ is a movable piece which stops or allows the passage of fluid.

clock	meter	switch	valve	gauge
☐ a)	☐ b)	☐ c)	☐ d)	☐ e)

26 Which word has the incorrect spelling?

accomplish	assignment	consultant	tasteful	goverment
☐ a)	☐ b)	☐ c)	☐ d)	☐ e)

27 Which word is the odd one out?

mock	artificial	genuine	assumed	fictitious
☐ a)	☐ b)	☐ c)	☐ d)	☐ e)

28 If the first word is 'The,' what is the eighth word when these words make a proper sentence?

The word is a describe to state perfection of Utopia.

perfection	state	Utopia	things	word
☐ a)	☐ b)	☐ c)	☐ d)	☐ e)

29 The number of times an event happens at regular intervals is called its ___.

fibrillation	waves	average	frequency	timing
☐ a)	☐ b)	☐ c)	☐ d)	☐ e)

30 Which word has the incorrect spelling?

corrupt	managable	depressing	unnerving	consensus
☐ a)	☐ b)	☐ c)	☐ d)	☐ e)

31 Which word is the odd one out?

patronise	endorse	impugn	espouse	defend
☐ a)	☐ b)	☐ c)	☐ d)	☐ e)

32 What is the last word in this jumbled sentence when it is in the proper order?

shells fossils and bones include animals of.

fossils	of	include	animals	shells
☐ a)	☐ b)	☐ c)	☐ d)	☐ e)

33   The ubiquitous spirit worshipped by the Incas thus ___ everything.

destroyed	invaded	pervaded	owned	idolised
☐ a)	☐ b)	☐ c)	☐ d)	☐ e)

34   Which word has the incorrect spelling?

opening	unnecesarily	grievously	openness	benefited
☐ a)	☐ b)	☐ c)	☐ d)	☐ e)

35   Which word is the odd one out?

virtuoso	wizard	maestro	prodigy	disciple
☐ a)	☐ b)	☐ c)	☐ d)	☐ e)

36   What is the last word in this jumbled sentence when it is in the proper order?

depends the upon factors from distance sea climate such as.

climate	factor	depends	sea	distance
☐ a)	☐ b)	☐ c)	☐ d)	☐ e)

Answers

1 b	**10** a	**19** c	**28** a
2 a	**11** c	**20** b	**29** d
3 d	**12** e	**21** e	**30** b
4 c	**13** b	**22** e	**31** c
5 d	**14** b	**23** a	**32** d
6 e	**15** d	**24** c	**33** c
7 a	**16** a	**25** d	**34** b
8 b	**17** c	**26** e	**35** e
9 e	**18** b	**27** c	**36** d

Scoring

Number right minus number wrong = _____

Plus 4 aged under 16, plus 2 if aged 17–20   + _____

Score on the test = _____

Use the following table to convert your test score to a score out of 10 or 'sten score'. You can then enter your 'sten score' in the chart on page 234.

Test score	1–8	9	10–12	13–15	16–18	19–21	22–24	25–27	28–30	31+
Sten score	1	2	3	4	5	6	7	8	9	10

TEST 20

VOCABULARY

This is a test of your understanding of words. You are given a word and have to say which one of the alternatives is closest in meaning to it. You have to place a tick in the correct box. Look at the examples below.

Examples

1	OWN	2	ADD
	☐ a) possess		☐ a) subtract
	☐ b) unpaid		☐ b) count
	☐ c) disown		☐ c) duke
	☐ d) landlord		☐ d) new

In Example 1, to 'possess' means the same as to 'own'. If you think of a sentence with the word own in, you will find that the word possess could replace it. For example, 'I *own* a car – I *possess* a car.' 'Unpaid' means 'owing', not to 'own'. 'Disown' means the opposite of to 'own'. Landlord means an 'owner', not to 'own'. 'Own' and 'possess' are verbs, whilst 'unpaid' is an adjective; 'disown' is a verb, but means the opposite of 'own', and 'landlord' is a noun.

In Example 2, 'subtract' is the opposite of 'add', although it is a verb, as 'add' is a verb. 'Duke' is a noun, but does not mean 'add'. 'New' means 'fresh', and therefore could be added, but it would not be able to replace the word 'add' in a sentence. In any case, 'fresh' is an adjective. Both 'add' and 'count' are verbs. 'Count' is the answer, because it is almost identical in meaning to 'add' and could easily replace it in a sentence, for example, 'You should *add* up your money – You should *count* up your money.' It does not matter that 'count' can have other meanings, for example, as a noun in 'The count and countess were invited to the palace.'

You can do the items in any order you like, although the questions get increasingly difficult. Do not mark this book if it is not your own, but record your answers and any working out you need to do on separate paper. If you wish to gain an estimate of your aptitude, record the number of the question you are on after exactly 5 minutes. Otherwise, you can have as much time as you want to do this test, but it is probably not worth spending any longer than 5 minutes, as you will find that you either know the meanings of the words or you do not.

Timed test: 5 minutes

Place a tick in the box of the alternative that is closest in meaning to the word in capitals.

1 BAD
- ☐ a) evil
- ☐ b) angel
- ☐ c) good
- ☐ d) ban

2 WET
- ☐ a) appetite
- ☐ b) strong
- ☐ c) watery
- ☐ d) dry

3 CHIEF
- ☐ a) mainly
- ☐ b) minor
- ☐ c) head
- ☐ d) unimportant

4 CHOP
- ☐ a) rough
- ☐ b) duty
- ☐ c) stormy
- ☐ d) divide

5 SOFT
- ☐ a) harsh
- ☐ b) undemanding
- ☐ c) contact
- ☐ d) comfort

6 GOWN
- ☐ a) sack
- ☐ b) shout
- ☐ c) robe
- ☐ d) about

7 IMAGINARY
- ☐ a) realistic
- ☐ b) bleak
- ☐ c) trance
- ☐ d) dreamy

8 ACTIVE
- ☐ a) mobile
- ☐ b) baffle
- ☐ c) rigid
- ☐ d) motion

9 PIERCE
- ☐ a) puncture
- ☐ b) stung
- ☐ c) loud
- ☐ d) stabbing

10 INVALUABLE
- ☐ a) worthless
- ☐ b) valuable
- ☐ c) variable
- ☐ d) cheap

11 ADAPT

- [ ] a) convert
- [ ] b) flexible
- [ ] c) inflexible
- [ ] d) transformation

12 IMPARTIAL

- [ ] a) connected
- [ ] b) detached
- [ ] c) involved
- [ ] d) unconcern

13 REPUTABLE

- [ ] a) infamous
- [ ] b) supposed
- [ ] c) good
- [ ] d) stature

14 LIGHTEN

- [ ] a) discover
- [ ] b) darken
- [ ] c) illumine
- [ ] d) weak

15 GROUNDLESS

- [ ] a) justified
- [ ] b) background
- [ ] c) basis
- [ ] d) absurd

16 FASTEN

- [ ] a) affix
- [ ] b) untie
- [ ] c) holder
- [ ] d) thin

17 BARGAINING

- [ ] a) trafficking
- [ ] b) anticipate
- [ ] c) promise
- [ ] d) agree

18 WORRISOME

- [ ] a) reassuring
- [ ] b) unworried
- [ ] c) annoy
- [ ] d) perturbing

19 UNDERCURRENT

- [ ] a) undercharge
- [ ] b) atmosphere
- [ ] c) undermine
- [ ] d) belittle

20 SATANIC

- [ ] a) divine
- [ ] b) devil
- [ ] c) inhuman
- [ ] d) biting

21 PRICELESS
- [ ] a) prized
- [ ] b) cheap
- [ ] c) menu
- [ ] d) expense

22 MUTINOUS
- [ ] a) defiance
- [ ] b) uprising
- [ ] c) obedient
- [ ] d) turbulent

23 HOMELY
- [ ] a) mother
- [ ] b) domestic
- [ ] c) formal
- [ ] d) revered

24 FUNCTIONAL
- [ ] a) plain
- [ ] b) official
- [ ] c) decorative
- [ ] d) gathering

25 EXEMPT
- [ ] a) spared
- [ ] b) liable
- [ ] c) except
- [ ] d) illustrate

26 GALLANT
- [ ] a) cowardly
- [ ] b) escort
- [ ] c) courageousness
- [ ] d) polite

27 EXPRESSLY
- [ ] a) assert
- [ ] b) energetic
- [ ] c) particularly
- [ ] d) vaguely

28 DAPPER
- [ ] a) sloppy
- [ ] b) spry
- [ ] c) bespeckled
- [ ] d) dappled

29 COGNIZANT
- [ ] a) unaware
- [ ] b) apprehension
- [ ] c) acquainted
- [ ] d) perception

30 PORTEND
- [ ] a) presage
- [ ] b) insignificant
- [ ] c) presentiment
- [ ] d) emblazon

31 BENEDICTION
- [ ] a) anathema
- [ ] b) benevolence
- [ ] c) munificence
- [ ] d) blessing

32 CONCOMITANT
- [ ] a) coincidental
- [ ] b) accidental
- [ ] c) incidental
- [ ] d) compressed

33 GUILELESS
- [ ] a) artful
- [ ] b) shame
- [ ] c) innocent
- [ ] d) transparent

34 CULMINATE
- [ ] a) crown
- [ ] b) peak
- [ ] c) begin
- [ ] d) pursue

35 EXONERATE
- [ ] a) absolution
- [ ] b) inflate
- [ ] c) incriminate
- [ ] d) vindicate

36 ICONOCLASTIC
- [ ] a) denunciatory
- [ ] b) credulity
- [ ] c) uncritical
- [ ] d) optimistic

37 IMPLICIT
- [ ] a) innuendo
- [ ] b) explicit
- [ ] c) latent
- [ ] d) stated

38 PENURIOUS
- [ ] a) paucity
- [ ] b) indigent
- [ ] c) dearth
- [ ] d) meditative

39 SPURIOUS
- [ ] a) authentic
- [ ] b) specious
- [ ] c) sordid
- [ ] d) dishevelled

40 TRANSMOGRIFY
- [ ] a) attitudinize
- [ ] b) traverse
- [ ] c) mutation
- [ ] d) metamorphose

Answers

1 a	9 a	17 a	25 a	33 c
2 c	10 b	18 d	26 d	34 b
3 c	11 a	19 b	27 c	35 d
4 d	12 b	20 c	28 b	36 a
5 b	13 c	21 a	29 c	37 c
6 c	14 c	22 d	30 a	38 b
7 d	15 d	23 b	31 d	39 b
8 a	16 a	24 a	32 c	40 d

Scoring

Number right minus number wrong = _____

Plus 2 aged under 16, plus 1 if aged 17–20   + _____

Score on the test =   _____

Use the following table to convert your test score to a score out of 10 or 'sten score'. You can then enter your 'sten score' in the chart on page 234.

Test score	1–3	4–6	7–9	10–13	14–17	18–22	23–25	26–28	29–31	32+
Sten score	1	2	3	4	5	6	7	8	9	10

VERBAL PRECISION

This test is to see how well you understand words and whether you can use them correctly. You are given a word or a pair of words. You have to select the word that fits best from the alternatives given. For each question there are alternative answers. Underline the correct answer. The first one has been done to show you how.

Examples

1   Which word has the closest meaning to Grave?

   a) <u>Serious</u>   b) Gravity   c) Needy   d) Detain

2   Which word is most nearly the opposite to Retreat?

   a) Study   b) Defend   c) <u>Advance</u>   d) Walking

In Example 1, of the options given, the word that is nearest in meaning to 'Grave' is 'Serious' so a) is underlined. In Example 2, the answer is c) 'Advance'.

In Example 1, 'grave' can have more than one meaning. It can mean where someone is buried, for example. It can also mean 'to scrape out', although this meaning is not used much these days. But if you look at the alternative answers, a) to d), none of these has to do with where a person is buried and none means 'to scrape'. 'Serious' means solemn, purposeful or important. 'Gravity' can also mean solemn or important, but can also have to do with the force that brings things to earth. 'Needy' has nothing to do with 'grave' because 'needy' means 'poor'. Although being 'needy' might be a 'grave' matter, it does not actually mean the same since being poor is not necessarily also serious. 'Detain' means to keep back or withhold, so does not have a similar meaning to 'grave'. So, of the alternatives, it seems that 'grave' could go with 'serious', but might also share a similar meaning to 'gravity'. How do you decide between 'serious' and 'gravity'? 'Grave' can be used as a describing word, as can 'serious'. Therefore, they are both being used as adjectives, whereas 'gravity' is the name of something. 'Gravity' can only be used as a noun. Therefore, 'grave' has the closest meaning to 'serious', so a) is the answer.

In Example 2, the opposite of 'retreat' would be to 'go forward' or 'advance'. 'Study' means something different. 'Defend' could be connected in some way with 'retreat', but is not the opposite. 'Walking' could describe both the manner of an 'advance' or a 'retreat'. It is not connected and neither is it the correct part of speech. Therefore, of the alternatives given, 'advance' is most nearly the opposite of 'retreat', so c) is the answer.

Do not mark this book if it is not your own, but record your answers and any working out you need to do on separate paper. If you wish to gain an estimate of your aptitude, record the number of the question you are on after exactly 8 minutes. Otherwise, take as long as you wish to complete the items.

Timed test: 8 minutes

1 Which word has the closest meaning to Seek?

a) Lose   b) Pursue   c) Hide   d) Cover

2 Which word is most nearly the opposite to Constant?

a) Soon   b) Unpredictable   c) Approved   d) Continual

3 Which word is closest in meaning to Majority?

a) Legal   b) Minority   c) Old   d) Most

4 Which word is closest in meaning to Ripe?

a) Fruit   b) Ready   c) Aged   d) Spoiled

5 Which word is closest in meaning to Recover?

a) Restore   b) Lose   c) Conscious   d) Make

6 Which word is closest in meaning to Envelop?

a) Post   b) Wrap   c) Letter   d) Show

7 Which word is most nearly the opposite in meaning to Hinder?

a) Former   b) Intercept   c) Encourage   d) Anticipate

8 Which word is most nearly the opposite of Gangling?

a) Soft   b) Quiet   c) Skinny   d) Dumpy

9 Which word is closest in meaning to Captivate?

a) Partner   b) Battle   c) Remove   d) Charm

10 Which word is closest in meaning to Obscure?

a) Parasol   b) Cloud   c) Clear   d) Blind

11 Which word is most nearly the opposite of Casual?

a) Feeble   b) Charming   c) Deliberate   d) Weak

12 Which word is closest in meaning to Catcall?

a) Praise   b) Scream   c) Whistle   d) Ovation

13 Which word is most nearly the opposite of Prohibit?

a) Refuse b) Smoke c) Untrue d) Allow

14 Which word is closest in meaning to Cast?

a) Class b) Tinge c) Species d) Barrel

15 Which word is closest in meaning to Debut?

a) Termination b) Young c) Premiere d) Speech

16 Which word is most nearly the opposite of Buoyant?

a) Rising b) Floating c) Sinking d) Marking

17 Which word is closest in meaning to Flotilla?

a) Swans b) Ships c) Heart problem d) Balloons

18 Which word is closest in meaning to Crown?

a) Adorn b) Cross c) Hill d) Jewel

19 Which word is most nearly the opposite of Gusto?

a) Fame b) Desire c) Apathy d) Appetite

20 Which word is closest in meaning to Saucy?

a) Lippy b) Politeness c) Container d) Interference

21 Which word is closest in meaning to Phoenix?

a) Bird b) Statue c) Phony d) Fire

22 Which word is closest in meaning to Ambrosia?

a) Food b) Dainty c) Jam d) Crab

23 Which word is closest in meaning to Developed?

a) Ungrudging b) Generous c) Cultivated d) Boundless

24 Which word is closest in meaning to Ridiculous?

a) Levity b) Jocular c) Wit d) Foolish

25 Which word is most nearly the opposite of Bent?

a) Bias b) Curved c) Leaning d) Impartial

26 Which word is closest in meaning to Manual?

    a) Primer   b) Note   c) Voucher   d) Disk

27 Which word is closest in meaning to Catch?

    a) Entangle   b) Extricate   c) Unravel   d) Sprawl

28 Which word is most nearly the opposite of Imprudent?

    a) Arbitrary   b) Judicious   c) Undiscerning   d) Subjective

29 Which word is closest in meaning to Retain?

    a) Dole   b) Mete   c) Portion   d) Keep

30 Which word is most nearly opposite to Loathing?

    a) Doting   b) Bungling   c) Hiding   d) Kindness

Answers

1 b	7 c	13 d	19 c	25 d
2 b	8 d	14 b	20 a	26 a
3 d	9 d	15 c	21 a	27 a
4 b	10 b	16 c	22 a	28 b
5 a	11 c	17 b	23 c	29 d
6 b	12 c	18 a	24 d	30 a

Scoring

Number right minus number wrong = _____

Plus 2 aged under 16, plus 1 if aged 17–20   + _____

Score on the test = _____

Use the following table to convert your test score to a score out of 10 or 'sten score'. You can then enter your 'sten score' in the chart on page 234.

Test score	1–2	3–4	5–6	7–9	10–12	13–15	16–17	18–19	20–21	22+
Sten score	1	2	3	4	5	6	7	8	9	10

Part Nine
Online testing

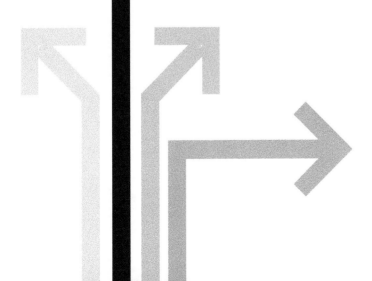

Online testing is used by organizations, firstly because the test has all the usual virtues of fairness in testing for purposes of assessment, selection and development and, secondly, because of the obvious advantages of ease, cost and quickness, thus benefitting both the organization as well as the test taker. The tests themselves are similar in content to paper tests, but it is wise to be familiar with online testing.

The Core intelligence test can be undertaken in this book and an extended version can be undertaken online. For the latter, go to **www.insight-tests.com/coreintelligencetest** and enter the code 71265 for your free version. Taking the test online will provide you with a) further experience of testing, and b) more information about yourself.

The purpose of Test 22 to establish a 'core' intelligence that is separate from a person's acquired skills or learning. This is also sometimes called 'pure' or 'underlying' intelligence.

It is generally the case that people who perform well on tests of 'core' intelligence are successful in adulthood, even if they have done less well in their early years in terms of academic attainment. This 'longer-term promise' is often revealed by higher scores on this test than other tests that assess conventional areas of aptitude. Testers may already have established that this type of test provides them with the kind of information useful in providing a guide to potential.

Although the look and form of the online test is the same as in this book, it is in some ways different, as it demands more of some psychological factors of persistence, and extended concentration. Therefore, your level of attainment may not be the same on both tests!

TEST 22

CORE INTELLIGENCE TEST

1	9	17	25	33	41
2	10	18	26	34	42
3	11	19	27	35	43
4	12	20	28	36	44
5	13	21	29	37	45
6	14	22	30	38	46
7	15	23	31	39	47
8	16	24	32	40	48

From the shapes in the chart, write the number of the shape that comes next in the line below:

Example 1

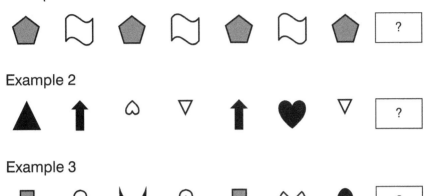

Example 2

Example 3

Answers to examples

Example 1

The figures go – white, grey, white, grey, so the next figure will be <u>white</u>. The drawings go – pentagon, wave, pentagon, wave, so the next figure will be a <u>wave</u>. Therefore, the next item will be – a <u>white wave</u>, which is number 21, as written in the box below:

       | 21 |

Example 2

There are two large figures, then two small ones, so the next figure must be <u>small</u>. There are two black figures and then two white figures, so the next figure will be <u>white</u>. Then there is a triangle, arrow and heart, so next in line after the last figure in the line will be an <u>arrow</u>. A <u>small, white arrow</u> is number 25 as shown below:

       | 25 |

Example 3

Every third figure is a large one, so the next figure, the second in the sequence, must be <u>small</u>. The colour sequence is – grey, white, black, white – so the next figure will be <u>white</u>. The figure sequence is – small square, pie, moon, pie – so the next figure will be a <u>pie</u>. The answer that should be written in the box is a <u>small, white pie</u>, as shown below:

There are many ways to do this test, so that you do not have to follow the method of sequences, as described above, although most people do. It may be useful to have a sheet of paper to hand in order to make a note of the sequences as you work out the scheme, which saves you having to hold all the information in your mind, although this method may be slower than perceiving what comes next by using your own method. You may prefer to see the shapes as 'down' or 'up' rather than 'large' or 'small', or you may prefer not to label them at all.

You will require a pen or pencil to record your answer, but use a separate sheet of paper if this book does not belong to you. In this case, it may be best to write down the numbers, 1 to 20, before you start the test so that this does not reduce the overall time you are allowed to do the test. You can time yourself accurately with a stop watch so stop on the question you are on after exactly eight minutes. If you are simply doing the test to gain familiarity with this process, take as long as you wish on all the items.

On this test you have to find the item that would come next on the right at the end of the sequence. Choose from the items in the reference table on page 226 and write your answer in the box or on a separate sheet of paper.

Timed test: 8 minutes

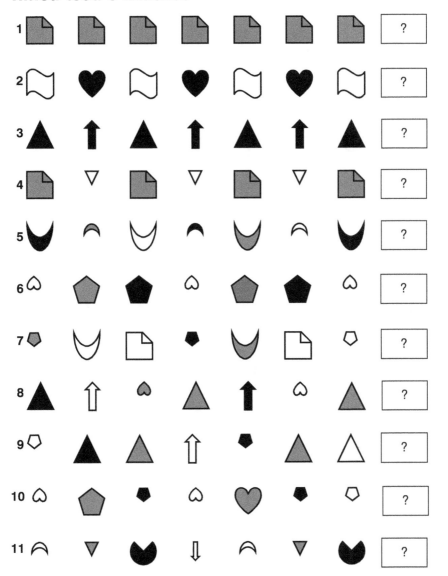

Answers

1 38	2 3	3 1	4 31	5 44
6 40	7 4	8 33	9 1	10 35
11 25	12 33	13 15	14 15	15 6
16 4	17 30	18 18	19 31	20 1

Scoring

Number right = _____
Minus number wrong = _____
Score = _____
Use the following table to convert your test score to a score out of 10 or 'sten score'. You can then enter your score in the chart on page 234

Test score	1	2	3	4–6	7–10	9–11	12–14	15–16	17–18	19–20
Sten score	1	2	3	4	5	6	7	8	9	10

Explanations

1   Large, large, large... so, large. Grey, grey, grey... so, grey. Square, square, square... so, square.
2   Large, large, large... so, large. White, black, white, black, white... so, black. Wave, heart, wave, heart, wave... so, heart.
3   Large, large, large... so, large. Black, black, black... so, black. Triangle, arrow, triangle, arrow, triangle... so, arrow.
4   Large, small, large, small... so, small. Grey, white, grey, white, grey... so, white. Square, triangle, square, triangle, square... so, triangle.
5   Large, small, large, small, large... so, small. Black, grey, white, black... so, grey. Moon, moon, moon... so, moon.
6   Small, large, large, small... so, large. White, grey, black, white... so, grey. Heart, pentagon, pentagon, heart... so, pentagon.
7   Small, large, large... so, large. Grey, white, white, black... so, black. Pentagon, moon, square, pentagon... so, moon.
8   Large, large, small... so, large. Black, white, grey, grey... so, grey. Triangle, arrow, heart, triangle... so, arrow.
9   Small, large, large, large... so, large. White, black, grey... so, black. Pentagon, triangle, triangle, arrow... so, arrow.
10   Large, small, small... so, large. White, grey, black... so, grey. Pentagon, pentagon, heart, heart... so, heart.

11   Small, small, small, large… so, small. White, white, grey, black… so, white. Moon, triangle, pie, arrow… so, arrow.

12   Large, large, small, small, small… so, large. White, grey, black, black… so, grey. Arrow, moon, heart, wave, wave… so, arrow.

13   Large, small, small, small… so, small. Black, black, grey, white, grey… so, black. Square, triangle, square, pie… so, triangle.

14   Small, small, small, large, large… so, small. Black, black, grey, white… so, black. Square, square, triangle, moon, triangle… so, triangle.

15   Large, large, large, small, small… so, large. Grey, grey, black, white… so, black. Triangle, moon, square, heart… so, square.

16   Large, large, large, small, small… so, large. White, grey, black, grey… so, black. Moon, moon, triangle, moon, heart… so, moon.

17   Small, large, small, large… small. Grey, grey, white, white, black, white… so, white. Pie, heart, pentagon, arrow, square, arrow, pie… so, square.

18   Small, large, two small, large… so, large. Black, white, two black, white… so, white. Wave, pentagon, heart, pie… so, pie.

19   Large, small, large, two small, large, three small, large… then four small, so small. Black, grey, grey, white, grey… so, white. Triangle, heart, pie, heart… so, triangle.

20   Small, two large, two small, large, small, two large, two small, large, small, two large…so, large. Grey, black, grey, white, black, white, black… so, black. Pentagon, arrow, pentagon, triangle, arrow, triangle…so, arrow.

Part Ten

Dispositional aptitude

This test assesses aptitudes in a different way from other tests in this book – whereas aptitudes of underlying intelligence are related to problem solving, 'disposition' is about behaviours used to accomplish tasks and deal with people; it is, effectively, problem solving, but using your genetic inheritance and emotional understanding.

Therefore, 'disposition' is used to describe your evolved, natural style in dealing with everyday situations. The results may assist you in changing your behaviour in ways you may prefer or assist you in changing your situation to another that may suit your better.

The test also allows you to check whether others perceive you in the same ways you perceive yourself. This can be used to clarify misunderstanding between people who work or live together.

In which situations do you feel are you more comfortable, satisfied or successful? The situations in which you feel you are most naturally yourself are the ones in which you experience most fulfilment. It follows that they are also the ones in which you feel most motivated. Therefore, it makes sense to aim to be in those situations where you can best exploit your dispositional aptitudes.

TEST 23

DISPOSITIONAL APTITUDE TEST

In this test you have to tick the statement that describes the way you usually feel or behave. (If you are completing the test on someone else it is how that person feels or behaves.)

You must choose one of the statements even though on some occasions the other statement could possibly also be true. Tick the statement that, on balance, feels right.

Of the two alternative statements, both are equally 'good' or 'correct'. Neither is 'bad' or 'wrong'. The more honest you are, the more valuable the analysis will be.

This test is not timed. No more than a few seconds is necessary with each item.

Start as soon as you are ready.

1 When fate suddenly deals me a blow I:

☐ a) never doubt that I can meet the challenge

☐ b) dwell on how I should have avoided it

2 I would prefer my work to:

☐ a) give me contact with lots of people all the time

☐ b) allow me to work by myself

3 When I have to travel to keep an appointment:

☐ a) I do my utmost to get there on time or even earlier

☐ b) I do not worry even if I am a bit late

4   I am better at:

☐   a) proposing an idea

☐   b) organizing a schedule

5   I like a work situation:

☐   a) when just one person arranges the way things are done

☐   b) when everybody arranges the way things are done

6   When I have an opinion that does not agree with everyone else:

☐   a) I do not hesitate to say why I see things differently

☐   b) I tend to keep things to myself

7   In a room full of strangers I:

☐   a) frequently am the one who will 'break the ice'

☐   b) tend to wait to see what somebody else does

8   I feel irritated if interrupted when concentrating upon an important matter:

☐   a) Tends to be true, especially if it's at a 'critical moment'

☐   b) No, because I welcome a diversion

9   I would prefer to read:

☐   a) about the life of a novelist or poet

☐   b) about the difficulties of exploring the floor of the ocean

10   People who work together are happier when:

☐   a) they know what they individually have to do

☐   b) they are aware of each other's feelings

11   If asked to take charge of a big event that I had never done before:

☐   a) I am willing to have a go

☐   b) I consider whether I have the ability to do it properly

12   During a break at work I would most likely be found :

☐   a) chatting with at least two people or a group

☐   b) having time to myself or with just someone I knew well

13   I prefer to:
☐   a) establish a plan
☐   b) see what happens

14   I would prefer to join:
☐   a) an amateur dramatics group
☐   b) an internet investment group

15   If there is no time left to deal with a very urgent matter, I prefer to:
☐   a) do it without having people discuss their doubts
☐   b) discuss people's doubts first

16   I like to have new things happen so I am kept 'on my toes'.
☐   a) Yes
☐   b) No

17   When it is suggested that a group of people should be formed:
☐   a) I always see more advantage in getting together
☐   b) I always see more disadvantage in getting together

18   I tend to think that:
☐   a) getting the details correct is the best way to proceed
☐   b) if matters are proceeding well details do not matter

19   I would prefer to:
☐   a) discuss a novel
☐   b) repair a broken machine

20   I am more likely to deal with the difficulties that arise by:
☐   a) pushing people to overcome them
☐   b) listening to what people say

21   After I make decisions rapidly:
☐   a) I forget it and get on with the next problem
☐   b) I am fearful that things may turn out badly

22   When asked to join a group activity I:

☐   a) am excited about new people or the opportunity

☐   b) doubtful about changing plans or strangers

23   In terms of safety and security:

☐   a) I keep checking over matters in my mind

☐   b) I do what is necessary and then feel relaxed about matters

24   I would be better at:

☐   a) creating an abstract painting

☐   b) drawing up a plan for a kitchen

25   In regard to the statement, 'The end justifies the means':

☐   a) I tend to agree

☐   b) I tend to disagree

26   If asked to take on an important new task, for which I am not ready, I think:

☐   a) "This could be humiliating."

☐   b) "I may look foolish, but I'll have a go."

27   I prefer to:

☐   a) establish just a few relationships I can be certain of

☐   b) extend my friends and contacts all the time

28   If I am going to attend an important meeting or interview I:

☐   a) react to the situation as I find it

☐   b) plan for what might happen as thoroughly as possible

29   I am more excited thinking about:

☐   a) possible methods of space travel

☐   b) finding a way towards spiritual awareness

30   People work harder when they are driven by:

☐   a) love

☐   b) hate

31 Before speaking I like to be sure that what I say will be appreciated:
- [ ] a) Agree
- [ ] b) Disagree

32 When invited to a group activity I am:
- [ ] a) unsure whether I really want to go
- [ ] b) happy not to be left out

33 I think that:
- [ ] a) if I cannot remember something it is unlikely to be important
- [ ] b) in case I forget it is useful to list important things to be done

34 I prefer to create something that can be:
- [ ] a) useful to people in their everyday living
- [ ] b) admired as a work of art

35 Success depends a lot upon trust between people:
- [ ] a) I tend to agree
- [ ] b) I tend to disagree

36 As far as I am concerned I:
- [ ] a) find it difficult to be sure what will satisfy me
- [ ] b) change things I am not satisfied with

37 When a group of people want somebody to be the leader I am likely:
- [ ] a) hold myself back
- [ ] b) to volunteer

38 Generally I:
- [ ] a) react to circumstances as they arise
- [ ] b) try to avoid unforeseen surprises

39 In the future the world's problems are more likely to be solved by:
- [ ] a) technology
- [ ] b) emotional understanding

40   Listening to the thoughts and feelings of everybody sharing a job:

☐   a) makes progress easier

☐   b) delays progress

41   When people doubt I can do something beyond what I have ever done before:

☐   a) I take their views into account

☐   b) I am determined to do better than expected

42   My preferred way of communicating would be to:

☐   a) write a letter or talk to people individually

☐   b) get everybody together and have a discussion

43   I think that people work better:

☐   a) when they can be spontaneous

☐   b) when they are clear about what they have to do

44   I tend to make up my mind by:

☐   a) weighing up one fact against the other

☐   b) the overall impression I have gained

45   If my boss told me of the difficulties they had it would make my job:

☐   a) easier

☐   b) more difficult

46   Self-doubt holds me back:

☐   a) Yes or sometimes

☐   b) No or only rarely

47   I make an effort to:

☐   a) keep work relationships separate from leisure time

☐   b) meet people I work with out of work as well

48   I would cope with worries or problems:

☐   a) by doing something different

☐   b) through orderliness and efficiency

49 My first question to an 'alien' from outer space would be:

☐ a) "How did you get here?"

☐ b) "What do you want?"

50 I believe that understanding people's attitudes and values:

☐ a) is essential when people are working together

☐ b) gets in the way of getting on with the work

Marking the test

In the table below, tick each box that agrees with your answer. For example if your answer to Question 1 was **a**, tick the box. If your answer was **b**, leave the box blank. Then add up the number of ticks in each column. For example the total of ticks in Column 1 will give your score out of ten for Action.

	1 a ☐	2 a ☐	3 a ☐	4 a ☐	5 a ☐
	6 a ☐	7 a ☐	8 a ☐	9 a ☐	10 a ☐
	11 a ☐	12 a ☐	13 a ☐	14 a ☐	15 a ☐
	16 a ☐	17 a ☐	18 a ☐	19 a ☐	20 a ☐
	21 a ☐	22 a ☐	23 a ☐	24 a ☐	25 a ☐
	26 b ☐	27 b ☐	28 b ☐	29 b ☐	30 b ☐
	31 b ☐	32 b ☐	33 b ☐	34 b ☐	35 b ☐
	36 b ☐	37 b ☐	38 b ☐	39 b ☐	40 b ☐
	41 b ☐	42 b ☐	43 b ☐	44 b ☐	45 b ☐
	46 b ☐	47 b ☐	48 b ☐	49 b ☐	50 b ☐
Totals					
	Action	Participation	Organization	Intellection	Realization

You now have your scores for five dispositional 'factors'. Next, mark your score for each factor with a tick on the chart below or, if you prefer, circle the number.

Disposition chart

Action	Reflective	0 1 2 3 4 – 5 6 7 8 9 10	Spontaneous
Participation	Independent	0 1 2 3 4 – 5 6 7 8 9 10	Social
Organization	General	0 1 2 3 4 – 5 6 7 8 9 10	Precise
Intellection	Logical	0 1 2 3 4 – 5 6 7 8 9 10	Intuitive
Realization	Sensitive	0 1 2 3 4 – 5 6 7 8 9 10	Tough

Description of the five factors

The actual words that best describe you may be in those provided, but there are many other words that lie within each group that are not given here that might describe you more accurately. Your own experience of your behaviour and how others perceive you will be the best guide as to where you would place yourself on each scale and what each factor means to you.

Action: Your reaction to difficulty

Reflective (scores 0–4)
thoughtful, cautious, self-doubting, anxious, considered, introspective
Spontaneous (scores 6–10)
impulsive, uninhibited, hasty, impetuous, reckless, thoughtless

Participation: Your behaviour with people

Independent (scores 0–4)
self-reliant, self-contained, unallied, separate, assured, unconnected
Social (scores 6–10)
popular, gregarious, public, familiar, neighbourly, companionable

Organization: Your approach to a task

General (scores 0–4)
adaptable, changeable, unsteady, fluctuating, versatile, variable
Precise (scores 6–10)
exact, strict, definite, finicky, fastidious, rigorous

Intellection: Your style of thinking

Logical (scores 0–4)
reasoning, objective, rational, factual, analytical, unemotional
Intuitive (scores 6–10)
feeling, instinctual, insight, abstract, empathic, sentimental

Realization: Your method of achieving

Sensitive (scores 0–4)

delicate, emotional, receptive, understanding, easily affected

Tough (scores 6–10)

strong, insensitive, hardy, thick-skinned, indifferent, firm

The effect of two factors upon motivation

Each factor can combine with others, as shown below. When factor scores are high or low it will be clear which situations are preferred. If one or both factor scores are average (score 5) or around average (say scores 4 or 6) then you may find it is possible to tolerate situations described by either of the factors, provided those situations are not extreme.

Consider the pairs of scores below and see where your own scores lie. This will give you four situations having most relevance to you. Think how they may relate to your own situation.

1 Coping with difficulty and involvement with people

a Action 6–10, Participation 6–10

You are most motivated and effective in situations where you can be spontaneous and participative. Least motivated in situations where you are expected to be reflective and independent.

b Action 0–4, Participation 6–10

Most motivated and effective in situations where you can be reflective and participative. Least motivated in situations where you are expected to be spontaneous and independent.

c Action 6–10, Participation 0–4

Most motivated and effective in situations where you can be spontaneous and independent. Least motivated in situations where you are expected to be reflective and participative.

d Action 0–4, Participation 6–10

Motivated and effective in situations where you can be both reflective and independent. Least motivated in situations where you are expected to be both spontaneous and participative.

2   Coping with difficulty and approach to a task

a   Action 6–10, Organization 6–10
Most motivated and effective in situations where you can be both spontaneous and detailed. Least suited to situations where you are expected to be both reflective and general.

b   Action 0–4, Organization 6–10
Most motivated and effective in situations where you can be both reflective and detailed. Least suited to situations where you are expected to be both spontaneous and general.

c   Action 6–10, Organization 0–4
You are most motivated and effective in situations where you can be both spontaneous and general. Least suited to situations in which you are expected to be both reflective and detailed.

d   Action 0–4, Organization 0–4
Most motivated and effective in situations where you can be both reflective and general. Least suited to situations where you are expected to be both spontaneous and detailed.

3   Coping with difficulty and style of thinking

a   Action 6–10, Intellection 6–10
Most motivated and effective in situations where you can be both spontaneous and intuitive. Least suited to situations where you are expected to be both logical and reflective.

b   Action 0–4, Intellection 6–10
Most motivated and effective in situations where you can be both reflective and intuitive. Least motivated in situations where you are expected to be both spontaneous and logical.

c   Action 6–10, Intellection 0–4
Most motivated and effective in situations where you can be both spontaneous and logical. Least motivated in situations where you can be both reflective and intuitive.

d   Action 0–4, Intellection 0–4
Most motivated and effective in situations where you can be both reflective and logical. Least motivated in situations where you are expected to be both spontaneous and intuitive.

4   Coping with difficulty and way of achieving

a   Action 6–10, Realization 6–10
Most motivated and effective in situations where you can be both sponta-neous and tough. Least motivated in situations where you are expected to be both reflective and sensitive.

b   Action 0–4, Realization 6–10
Most motivated and effective in situations where you can be both reflec-tive and tough. Least motivated in situations where you are expected to be both spontaneous and sensitive.

c   Action 6–10, Realization 0–4
Most motivated and effective in situations where you can be both sponta-neous and sensitive. Least motivated in situations where you are expected to be both reflective and tough.

d   Action 0–4, Realization 0–4
Most motivated and effective in situations where you can be both reflec-tive and sensitive. Least motivated in situations in which you are expected to be both spontaneous and tough.

5   Involvement with people and approach to a task

a   Participation 6–10, Organization 6–10
Most motivated and effective in situations where you can be both partici-pative and detailed. Least motivated in situations where you are expected to be both independent and general.

b   Participation 6–10, Organization 0–4
Most motivated and effective in situations where you can be both partici-pative and general. Least motivated in situations where you are expected to be both independent and detailed.

c   Participation 0–4, Organization 6–10
Most motivated and effective in situations where you can be both inde-pendent and detailed. Least motivated in situations where you are expected to be both participative and general.

d   Participation 0–4, Organization 0–4
Most motivated and effective in situations where you can be both inde-pendent and general. Least motivated in situations where you are expected to be both participative and detailed.

6   Involvement with people and style of thinking

a   Participation 6–10, Intellection 6–10
Most motivated and effective in situations where you can be both participative and intuitive. Least motivated in situations where you are expected
to be both independent and logical.

b   Participation 6–10, Intellection 0–4
Most motivated and effective in situations where you can be both participative and logical. Least motivated in situations where you are expected
to be both independent and intuitive.

c   Participation 0–4, Intellection 6–10
Most motivated and effective in situations where you can be both independent and intuitive. Least motivated in situations where you are
expected to be both participative and logical.

d   Participation 0–4, Intellection 0–4
Most motivated and effective in situations where you can be both independent and logical. Least motivated in situations where you are expected
to be both participative and intuitive.

7   Involvement with people and way of achieving

a   Participation 6–10, Realization 6–10
Most motivated and effective in situations where you can be both participative and tough. Least motivated in situations where you are expected to
be both independent and sensitive.

b   Participation 6–10, Realization 0–4
Most motivated and effective in situations where you can be both participative and sensitive. Least motivated in situations where you are expected
to be both independent and tough.

c   Participation 0–4, Realization 6–10
Most motivated and effective in situations where you can be both independent and tough. Least motivated in situations where you are expected
to be both participative and sensitive.

d   Participation 0–4, Realization 0–4
Most motivated and effective in situations where you can be both independent and sensitive. Least motivated in situations where you are
expected to be both participative and tough.

8   Approach to a task and style of thinking

a   Organization 6–10, Intellection 6–10
Most motivated and effective in situations where you can be both detailed and intuitive. Least motivated in situations where you are expected to be both general and logical.

b   Organization 6–10, Intellection 0–4
Most motivated and effective in situations where you can be both detailed and logical. Least motivated in situations where you are expected to be both general and intuitive.

c   Organization 6–10, Intellection 6–10
Most motivated and effective in situations where you can be both general and intuitive. Least motivated in situations where you are expected to be both detailed and logical.

d   Organization 0–4, Intellection 0–4
Most motivated and effective in situations where you can be both general and logical. Least motivated in situations where you are expected to be both detailed and intuitive.

9   Approach to a task and way of achieving

a   Organization 6–10, Realization 6–10
Most motivated and effective in situations where you can be both detailed and tough. Least motivated in situations where you are expected to be both general and sensitive.

b   Organization 6–10, Realization 0–4
Most motivated and effective in situations where you can be both detailed and sensitive. Least motivated in situations where you are expected to be both general and tough.

c   Organization 0–4, Realization 6–10
Most motivated and effective in situations where you can be both general and tough. Least motivated in situations where you are expected to be both detailed and sensitive.

d   Organization 0–4, Realization 0–4
Most motivated and effective in situations where you can be both general and sensitive. Least motivated in situations where you are expected to be both detailed and tough.

10   Style of thinking and way of achieving

a   intellection 6–10, Realization 6–10
Most motivated and effective in situations where you can be both intuitive and tough. Least motivated in situations where you are expected to be both logical and sensitive.

b   intellection 6–10, Realization 0–4
Most motivated and effective in situations where you can be both intuitive and sensitive. Least motivated in situations where you are expected to be both logical and tough.

c   Intellection 0–4, Realization 6–10
Most motivated and effective in situations where you can be both logical and tough.
Least motivated in situations where you are expected to be both intuitive and sensitive.

d   Intellection 0–4, Realization 0–4
Most motivated and effective in situations where you can be both logical and sensitive. Least motivated in situations where you are expected to be both intuitive and tough.

Suggestions for interpretation

The analysis of dispositional aptitude is complex because:

a)   The scores and the descriptions are not judgemental. There is nothing 'better than' or 'worse than' or 'good' or 'poor' about them. They are just descriptions intended to provide insight into how and in what situations dispositional may be used most effectively.

b)   Your score on the test will have a different qualitative value and meaning unique to you so it cannot be compared with someone else's score in the same way as an intelligence or ability test.

c)   Although you may typically behave more in one way rather than its opposite, you may also behave in the opposite way in certain circumstances.

d)   Although one of the factors may be more important to you than others, the conditions or circumstances in which that factor combines with one or, perhaps, all of the others is likely to be even more important.

e)   If you do not perceive the analysis to be exactly your perception, do not reject it out of hand, but use it as a basis for exploration. Ask yourself whether there might be more truth in it that you might sometimes think or whether some parts apply in some circumstances and not others.

f) Whilst high or low scores on each indicate pronounced behaviour, a middle score of 5 or close to 5 is likely to indicate that your disposition and therefore your behaviour can tend either way or perhaps encompass either end of the scale without being extreme. So, for example, you may be tolerant or able to adapt to circumstances or conditions that someone of a more extreme disposition may experience as not naturally suited to them.

g) Be open to the results and use the results to challenge your way of seeing your own or someone else's behaviour! Good questions for you are: 'How and in what way might this be true? If it is only partly true, what can be learnt from it?'

h) Ask others in what ways people perceive a result as being true or untrue. It is helpful if they will illustrate with examples of real events and situations. It is revealing to discover whether their perceptions are the same as yours and how they have gained the impression they have.

i) It is most helpful if another person has completed this test, either their perception of you or them. It is a valuable to see in what ways your results are the same or how different perceptions have arisen.

j) It can be valuable to discuss what it means to you both to have similarities or differences in your behaviours in terms of how you relate to each other and how you work together.

Comparative disposition chart

Use the chart below to mark with a circle or cross any differences or comparisons that may be important to you. It is most helpful if you discuss your scores and the scores of others together.

A) How I want to be.
(May be the same. If not, what do you do about it?)

B) What is expected in the situation I am in?
(How can you check you are correct about this?)

C) How I perceive others.
(Name...)

D) How others perceive me.
(Name...)

Action	Reflective	0 1 2 3 4 – 5 6 7 8 9 10	Spontaneous
Participation	Independent	0 1 2 3 4 – 5 6 7 8 9 10	Social
Organization	General	0 1 2 3 4 – 5 6 7 8 9 10	Precise
Intellection	Logical	0 1 2 3 4 – 5 6 7 8 9 10	Intuitive
Realization	Sensitive	0 1 2 3 4 – 5 6 7 8 9 10	Tough

You can make notes here of significant points from your personal reflection or from what you have learnt from others:

....
....
....
....
....
....

Combining the five dispositional aptitudes

How do all of your five factors factors interplay in whatever you may do – at work, at home, socially and in all spheres of your life? Depending upon the situation you are in, the weight or influence of any of the factors may alter. As a guide, the following are general interpretations to assist in thinking about and perhaps changing either your behaviour or those situations that make you feel you are behaving in a way that is not naturally motivating for you.

Find the *combined set* of dispositional factors that has most relevance to you from these:

1   Spontaneous, social, detailed, intuitive, tough

These can make you a good **campaign manager** especially in a creative atmosphere. Your purposefulness, grasp of the situation and vision the ultimate goal, your social skills and enthusiasm help you to win through when others may have given up. You are determined and controlling, your toughness and dynamism pushing for achievement. People will enjoy engaging in a task with you as they will find you stimulating and demanding, although they may need to recognize that you are less interested in their feelings than in getting the task done. If you are high on the spontaneous scale you will enjoy taking on new challenges or sorting out complex, difficult projects.

2   Reflective, social, detailed, intuitive, tough

You are likely to be a good **strategist** especially in a creative atmosphere. You consider matters seriously and in depth, pondering upon the consequences for the whole situation including the objective and the people involved. You will respond to people and win them over, sharing problems with them and explaining the hard decisions that may need to be made, which you certainly will not shrink from. In fact, though usually quite and friendly, you can be exacting about they way you want things done. You are good at coping with pressures, taking the time to think them through, and you will want to avoid taking rapid action.

3   Spontaneous, social, detailed, intuitive, sensitive

Your interpersonal skills combine with your enthusiasm, openness and commitment to make you a good **captain** especially in a creative situation in which people's skills are essential to getting things done. You can be effective in building something that inspires others and allows them to flourish as part of a joint effort. You perceive opportunities, but also pay attention to details, all the time maintaining communication between everybody involved. Where your spontaneity is high you will enjoy fast-paced roles.

4   Thoughtful, social, detailed, intuitive and sensitive.

You have insight, consideration and social skill that can combine to make you effective as a **guide or adviser**. You both see opportunities and work towards objectives carefully, all the while bearing in mind the impact that events can have upon those around you. You will probably not enjoy having a role that demands any ruthlessness or lack of consideration for others as this would conflict with your values and the equable basis upon which you relate to people. As a rule you like to encourage others in a cooperative effort.

5   **Spontaneous, social, detailed, logical and tough.**
These can make you a persuasive, even forceful, personality that is often seen in a **producer** or **executive**. The determination to push hard and get things done at all costs can motivate others who respond to your fast-pace and factual, concrete approach. You have plenty of social skill but are also businesslike and driven to achieve. Well prepared and capable, you usually have a rationale that is straightforward and focused upon results. You can have a manner that shows as impatience in situations that require subtlety in dealing with emotional issue that arise from your own conviction and confidence, so are usually suited to working among others who similarly thrive on rapid achievement.

6   **Thoughtful, social, detailed, logical and tough**
Your cautious and factual approach together with a talent for engaging with others makes you effective in **building firm foundations** and structures with people and undertaking tasks. People will know they can rely upon you skills and the fact that you have carefully weighed up and solved problems. The fact that you are unlikely to take risks is reassuring. At the same time, you can have a dogged approach that is less well suited to dealing with people's feelings than with the facts of the matter. You like to be in control and therefore feel uncomfortable if required to be reactive or impulsive.

7   **Spontaneous, social, detailed, logical and sensitive**
Your perceptive social skills and administrative aptitude make you effective as a **negotiator** or **arbitrator**. You enjoy taking the initiative and managing situations to bring out the talents that others have. You participate readily and know what is going on. You have a strong desire to achieve and have a factual and clear estimate of how to approach problems and overcome them. Whilst sensitive, you are also purposeful in working towards practical solutions. Your confidence and style suit you for demanding and sometimes wide ranging responsibilities.

8   **Reflective, social, detailed, logical and sensitive**
You have considerable empathy with others whilst also being knowledge-able and focused in what you do, these characteristics combining to make you as a **mediator** or **team player**. Though your task skills may well be impressive people are unlikely to feel intimidated, perceiving you as a capable colleague who will work with them to overcome problems. It will be important to you that you and others are treated in a way that fits with your own values. You will like to be involved with things that are technical but also have a cultural or social dimension.

9 **Spontaneous, social, general, intuitive, tough**

Your willingness and confidence in taking the initiative in open-ended situations in which ideas and commitment are important make you an able **persuader**. You are not necessarily forceful although there can be an element of ruthlessness at times in the way you are determined to achieve. You are not daunted by tough decisions and do not worry over much by what others might regard as pressure. You prefer others to deal with details, preferring to engage with the wider issues. You do not like routine much, preferring a creative environment where quick thinking and action are essential.

10 **Reflective, social, general, intuitive, tough**

You are good at meeting with others and working on ideas, often at short notice where decisions have to be made quickly without detailed analysis or consultation. Therefore your characteristics make you effective in **applying knowledge and providing flair**. Although you mix easily with people, you prefer their problems not to be a demanding part of what you want to achieve so that the social side of your relationships is not brought into conflict by the nature of your work. You may prefer to work with people but have the scope to make decisions largely in your own way in your own area of expertise.

11 **Spontaneous, social, general, intuitive sensitive**

Your confidence, perception and involvement with many things at many levels suggest that you are **open to ideas and change**. You are likely to have a good deal of confidence and can have a great impact upon others who will respond to you and find you easy to get on with you are often a stimulating companion. You are likely to develop many valuable contacts that you maintain over time. Your strengths come out most effectively in situations where your sensitive understanding of people and creative endeavour are both important.

12 **Reflective, social, general, intuitive, sensitive**

your understanding, even empathy, when dealing people as well as your involvement with ideas can make you an **idealist**. You are able to see many sides of an issue, especially the implications for those persons affected. People's personal and cultural values are important to you and you have principles that guide your own life and the way others should be treated. Although you can be an inspiration for others who may welcome your advice, you may experience uncertainty and therefore seek to resolve issues, make adjustments or gain experience in order to align yourself more closely with the quality of life that you seek.

13 **Spontaneous, social, general, logical, tough**
Your social confidence combines with a factual, hard-headed style is likely to make you an **achiever**. You like a good deal of freedom in the way you do things and are likely to known as someone who is capable of getting things done. In fact, you will probably not wait to be asked but will be pushing to get on with things. You like to achieve quickly and may be impatient when dealing with the 'niceties' of a situation. You show certainty that can appear opinionated or dismissive of people who do not see things your way. The fact that you are sociable does not mean that you are dependent upon others.

14 **Reflective, social, general, logical, tough**
Clarity of thought and consideration of the people around you imply that you are likely to be a sound **decision maker**. You show decisiveness through you ability to understand the fact of the matter without being overly focused on detail or burdened by sentiment. You are likely to be perceived as a good, reliable person to work with because you want to get on with things and at the same time will fit in with those who are undertaking the same task. You evaluate and take stock of situations, ultimately basing decisions less on feelings than upon facts.

15 **Spontaneous, social, general, logical, sensitive**
Able to get to know others quickly and grasping problems and issues quickly as well, so are likely to be seen as a **capable enthusiast**. You are very people oriented as you have both interpersonal skill and emotional understanding. You probably have learned that you need to relate to people with tact and insight if you are not to be seen as over demanding of their attention. There may be a danger of over enthusiasm or perhaps of over burdening yourself. You quickly grasp problems and how to deal with them, taking on many responsibilities, particularly in relating to people where you will identify opportunities for their development.

16 **Reflective, social, general, logical, sensitive**
Your reflective, objective and insightful characteristics are likely to make you a sound **friend and ally**. You weigh up matters with attention to how others are feeling and give your views with genuine concern to help and inform. You are well meaning but also sensible in not pushing any view before people are ready and with out trying to look clever or gain anything for yourself. You have the potential to create an enjoyable, supportive atmosphere. The way people live and work together will usually be as or more important to you than material achievement.

17   Spontaneous, independent, precise, intuitive, tough

Possessing confidence and self-reliance in thinking things through on your own, and applying yourself with purpose makes you an **authority**. You act quickly and incisively, which is effective in some circumstances where decisions have to be made quickly, but less so where others are involved as it is possible they may feel you are excluding them. You are likely to be knowledgeable and organized and like to do things in your own way, having the ability to make decisions in a firm, informed manner. You are likely to be less suited to a role requiring subtleties of empathy or tact.

18   Reflective, independent, detailed, intuitive, tough

Your careful, comprehensive, thinking – and focus, with which you balance creativity with attention to small essentials – all combine to form an independent judgement. You may be regarded as a shrewd ability or to be something of an **expert**. You are unlikely to be reliant upon others to form an opinion but rely upon your own knowledge and experience. Although you may be open to debate you may at an extreme be categorical or stubborn. The issues you seem best at dealing with are likely to be intellectual or material ones that do not involve you personally in emotional or social issues. As you are structured about the facts of matters, you can be effective as a detached advisor in business as well as other spheres.

19   Spontaneous, independent, detailed, intuitive and sensitive

You have the ability to perceive matters clearly and your optimism and clear sightedness can make you a good **problem resolver**. You are generally considerate and thoughtful but are not obviously very social, though you do take careful account of people's feelings. People will often want to include you more than you want, but when you choose to be with others you are supportive and companionable. Sometimes you may consider matters too deeply or take matters too much to heart but you seem able to resolve your doubts with sound sense, regard for others and attention to what is expected of you.

20   Reflective, independent, detailed, intuitive and sensitive

Generally introspective and seriously minded you are nevertheless a good **reader of situations**. You are alert to what is going on although you probably have too many self-doubts and take criticism or adversity too much too heart. People will trust your sincerity and loyalty. You feel things deeply and are always turning situations, possibilities and the past over in your mind. It is most important to you to establish mutually aware relationships with those you are with as you do not want to be in situations where people's regard for each other is not the highest priority.

21   Spontaneous, independent, detailed, logical, tough

You have talents in areas of knowledge and practice where your enthusiasm to achieve definite, objective goals will make you a formidable **technical expert**. You can be detached and penetrating, wanting to get to the nub of an issue. The service, skills or products that you can put in place will be useful as these are often measurable in terms of concrete achievements. You seem most suited to task oriented or specialized roles and less suited to those that require interpersonal or emotional awareness. In situations such as the latter you prefer to ignore them although your dealings with the task or similarly minded people will not bring you into very much contact with interpersonal issues. When focused on facts, you are self-reliant and resourceful.

22   Reflective, independent, detailed, logical and tough

You are self-reliant, objective, careful and intent upon getting what you do correct, so will be effective as a **specialist**. You are particularly strong with technical issues where your black-and-white approach to problem resolution comes into its own. You seem to be less naturally suited to dealing with emotional situations between people, being less able to define and establish what upsets people. You are not suited to a role requiring intuition or social flair, your preference being to work in your own way so that you can apply your skills and experience to the task – though this may well be as part of a team who share similar objectives.

23   Spontaneous, independent, detailed, logical and sensitive

You are thoughtful about all that you do whether working with others or applying yourself to your own interests, so are regarded as 'insightful'. Although not extrovert, you have a determination and confidence that makes you a high achiever. You may well have come from a technical education but then will like work in which you can use your skills on behalf of others. You reflect on issues, being concerned about the impact of these upon people whilst also using your own judgement to arrive at a rational view. Your actions are both orderly as well as balanced. Where you sometimes lack imagination you make up for in sympathy and endeavour.

24   Reflective, independent, detailed, logical and sensitive

You are cautious and thoughtful so are generally seen as both supportive as well as capable. You are tolerant of people and their difficulties although you may be inclined to keep matters to yourself, which may make people wish you were more outspoken. Your preference will be to apply yourself in technical, factual areas where you can specialize and be organized; you do not like matters to be vague or unfinished but feel more in control when you can establish a procedure or measurable achievement that you know will be appreciated by others. You will be perceived as very competent and with greater potential, although you may prefer the security as you may not want to push yourself so quickly than you feel unsure or exposed before you are prepared.

25   Spontaneous, independent, general, intuitive and tough

As you are self-reliant in so many ways – in relation to ideas, people and taking action – you are likely to be **creative**. You probably have little time for what others' want except in so far as they can support you in your project or passion. You have divergent interests and ideas, and are keen and energetic in expressing these. You may be more regarded as interesting or even inspiring than sympathetic or caring. You like to work with others who are willing to become involved and excited in a similar vision of creating something that people outside you or your immediate team will experience as impressive, valuable and worthwhile.

26   Reflective, independent, general, intuitive and tough

Using your own resources, especially your imagination, you are likely to be **artistic**. Because you prefer so much disposed to direct others, you will prefer to work in your own way. You feel that what you do is of the best quality when you are self-reliant and can make the crucial decisions yourself. You can be quite single-minded, even stubborn, about the way things should be done, but seem unsuited to dealing with criticism of your judgement or intuition. If in a team you are likely to prefer a specialist role in which you do not have to compromise upon your contribution so that it has a value that is attributable to your own expertise.

27   Spontaneous, independent, general, intuitive and sensitive

You are perceptive about both ideas and people so that, together with a self-assurance, you can be a discerning **adviser**. Knowledgeable and informed, you are interested in the application of theory to conceptual problems as well as to practical, human ones. You have an ability to comprehend the essentials of issues and a reassuring way of communicating these. You are likely to counsel and suggest rather than insist or be forceful. Your composure and ability to see beyond immediate issues can make you effective in giving direction to others in situations requiring a delicate awareness.

28   Reflective, independent, general, intuitive and sensitive

You have a contemplative nature, probably have many intellectual interests that and have a natural concern for others, all making you something of an empathetic **consultant**. You are more concerned with broad issues and the truth of matters rather than minor points of organization. You can become restless if there is no new challenge or when you find the behaviour of others incompatible with your own cultural or social principles. You listen sympathetically and your advice is likely to be appreciated, but you probably lack the emotional toughness to want to engage in gruelling, confrontational roles.

29   Spontaneousindependent, general, logical, tough

You do not need the support of people much and you have the factual, hard-headed approach that makes you **task-oriented**. You work out things for yourself, set your own goals and act on them. You are prepared to give direction to others with whom you appreciate the advantages of your disposition; you may well be regarded as someone who has the resolve and initiative to tackle problems others fear are too intractable or sensitive. You may be seen as uncaring even ruthless, but you may justify your actions by saying that these things have to be done. Nevertheless, it is likely that a fuller more inclusive communication with those around you could make you even more effective.

30   Reflective, independent, general, logical, tough

As you like to work in your own way on factual problems, which are within your own control, you will be good at **undertaking an assignment**. In relation to your skills or methods you can be persistent, even stubborn, about what you do or the way you do it. In this way you are much like a craftsperson, expert in their own area, who likes to be let alone to perform their skill without being overseen. You do not want to work closely with others except in circumstances in which their skills are required to complement your own. Often you do not see the point in giving others much explanation or may be unsure how worthwhile it may be to deal with them.

31   Spontaneous, independent, general, logical, sensitive

You have a self-reliant capability and are also aware of the implications of decisions upon others, so you have potential as a **manager**. Without being social, you yet have a composure and insight that suits situations in which you can work cooperatively with others. You would not be so suited to a hard driving role where you did not have others' support. Perhaps because you have an underlying shyness, you will welcome people as a resource and often get the best from them, though there are possibly times when you might be more effective if you confronted conflicts more directly. Your strong, deductive mind makes you quite formidable although it is possible that you allow yourself to be imposed upon; you respond readily, but some of what you do should perhaps have been carried out by those whose job it really is.

32   Reflective, independent, general, logical, sensitive

Well informed, intellectually curious, socially perceptive and aware, you are something of a **sensitive authority**. You have more awareness than may be obvious from your usual, fairly quiet style. People may expect that you would like to be more included or to have a more controlling role, but you preference is to be part of a more supportive or collegial group. Some lack of assurance or natural caution leads you to prefer a familiar respon-sibility among people you have learned you can rely upon and largely share your values. You can become restless in your situation if the level of mental challenge diminishes or if you find yourself in a group that is alien to your own cultural or social values.

Possible questions raised from the test and analysis

1 In what ways is my motivation suitable for the work I do or want to do?

2 In what ways does it matter that my disposition is different from the way others perceive me?

3 Discuss with one or more people in what ways do your perceptions of each other's behaviour differ?

4 What are the implications of perceived differences for the way we relate to or work with each other?

5 Do I want to change anything to feel more motivated and effective?

6 Have I resolved any possible areas of conflict either within myself or between others?

CALCULATING YOUR IQ

The IQ (intelligence quotient) scale is a familiar 'measuring stick' or 'ruler'; it allows a comparison with any other individual or with any other reference group. The use of IQ, or percentiles, which is equally easy for most people to understand, locates your performance on a scale that is the same for everyone.

Any particular test score makes little sense by itself. It has to be compared with a relevant population. A population may be any class of people, animals or objects that may be defined as relevant. For example, in medicine it might be helpful to check on the development of a newborn baby by comparing the weight of the baby with that of other newborn babies. Over time, data become available for an enormous number of newly born babies, so the mean (average) weight becomes a highly accurate representation of the population of babies.

As more data are acquired it is possible to become increasingly certain about how 'true' population statistics are. Because of the difficulty of testing large groups of people, statisticians and other researchers, including market researchers, often try to pinpoint a 'cross-section' of the entire population. Or they may target a particular population, such as a sample of twins, people in a certain income group or people who have passed accountancy examinations. For most tests, we refer to a sample of people who have taken the tests, referring to the sample as the 'population'. We make the assumption that the magnitude and variability of the sample is a true representation of the entire population, or the 'normal distribution'.

The normal distribution

If it were possible to test everybody in an entire population on a particular variable we assume that the scores would be dispersed about the mean in a

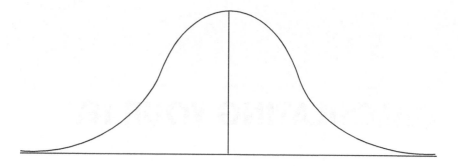

characteristic way that we refer to as 'normal'. Any sample or set of scores is assumed to be part of the normal distribution.

In the curve of normal distribution the base line represents the variable in question. It is usual to place the lowest number in the scale on the left side and the highest on the right. The highest point on the curve shows the mean or average point. So the greatest number of scores will be at the greatest magnitude. The mean could be drawn as a vertical line from the highest point down to the base line. About the mean, the two curves, that is, one on the left and one on the right of the mean, are symmetrical so that there is an equal magnitude of scores on both sides of the curve. Beneath any point on the curve the relative quantity or density of scores at that magnitude can be represented. Using the normal distribution allows us to place different sets of data on the same scale.

In this book effort has been made to include tests that will as far as possible reflect the curve of the normal distribution. In other words, the test gets harder as you proceed through it! At the end of each test, your result may be compared by reference to the chart of normal distribution.

Comparing your scores using the IQ

Your IQ is a number by which you can a) compare yourself with other people on any tests, and b) compare your own performance between the tests.

This book cannot measure your IQ with any great accuracy, as the conditions for measuring your IQ, as well as the information required to compare your intelligence with a satisfactory sample of people like you, are not available.

Why, then, provide a guide to IQ? First, because you are likely to find the exercise interesting for its own sake. Secondly, because the tests in this book are very similar to other tests used to measure intelligence, it enables a fuller comprehension of the entire process of intellectual measurement. Furthermore, an estimate of IQ provides a quick way of asking yourself whether you are going in a direction with your studies or in your career that will allow you to fully use your potential.

The IQ scale

Most IQ scales use the number 100 as an average. People with above average scores, say, above about 115 on appropriate tests, usually extend their schooling, obtaining vocational and technical qualifications.

People with stronger aptitudes are usually able to apply themselves to degree or professional courses. This group will, roughly, be the intellectual top 10 per cent and have an average IQ of 119. The top 5 per cent have an IQ around 125. If you are very good at the tests, you may have an IQ that is around 135, which puts you into the top 1 per cent.

Remember to interpret your own score only as a general guide. Your 'true' IQ will not be revealed unless you are compared with people of the same age, sex and relevant background. It is best to assume that your own IQ from the table provided here is likely to be only a baseline estimate. Use it to ask yourself whether you are achieving what you would expect at college or in your career. What tests should you use to calculate your IQ? It is possible to obtain an IQ on each one of the tests. The fairest estimate is probably to take the sum of several scores, then divide that number by the number of tests you have used.

Find your IQ by using the chart on the next page. Use your score out of 10 on any test and relate this to the IQ figures at the top.

IQ	100	105	110	115	120	125	130	135	140	145
ABSTRACT VISUAL										
1 Constructs	1	2	3	4	5	6	7	8	9	10
2 Sequences	1	2	3	4	5	6	7	8	9	10
3 Perceptual	1	2	3	4	5	6	7	8	9	10
ABSTRACT NUMERICAL										
4 Reasoning	1	2	3	4	5	6	7	8	9	10
5 Interpolation	1	2	3	4	5	6	7	8	9	10
ABSTRACT VERBAL										
6 Deduction	1	2	3	4	5	6	7	8	9	10
7 Analysis	1	2	3	4	5	6	7	8	9	10
PHYSICAL										
8 Dynamics	1	2	3	4	5	6	7	8	9	10
9 Tracing	1	2	3	4	5	6	7	8	9	10
SPATIAL										
10 Formation	1	2	3	4	5	6	7	8	9	10
11 3D tests	1	2	3	4	5	6	7	8	9	10
PRACTICAL NUMERICAL										
12 Reckoning	1	2	3	4	5	6	7	8	9	10
13 Arithmetic	1	2	3	4	5	6	7	8	9	10
14 Figure work	1	2	3	4	5	6	7	8	9	10
15 Number skills	1	2	3	4	5	6	7	8	9	10
16 Calculations	1	2	3	4	5	6	7	8	9	10
SYSTEMS										
17 Systems	1	2	3	4	5	6	7	8	9	10
18 Coding	1	2	3	4	5	6	7	8	9	10
PRACTICAL VERBAL										
19 Word usage	1	2	3	4	5	6	7	8	9	10
20 Vocabulary	1	2	3	4	5	6	7	8	9	10
21 Verbal precision	1	2	3	4	5	6	7	8	9	10
ONLINE TEST										
22 Core intelligence	1	2	3	4	5	6	7	8	9	10

As it can be misleading to try to calculate IQ from the score of a single test, use the following method to measure more accurately by using a number of tests, thus including some different aspects of intelligence. The chart is not absolutely accurate; because of the reasons given above and in the Introduction, it only intends to provide approximate guidance.

Calculating your overall IQ

(The space is for entering the number of tests used.)

Add sten scores from (_____) tests = _____

Divide by (_____) tests =   _____

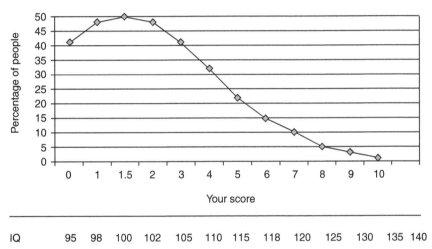

Chart of score and aptitude

Explanation: if, for example, you scored 7, only 10 per cent of people scored more highly; you are in the 'top 10 per cent' and the equivalent IQ is 120.

INDEX